MICHELE KENDALL

MONEY TALKS

Everything Your Parents Should Have Taught You About Saving and Spending (But Didn't)

First published by Platypus Publishing 2024

First edition

ISBN: 978-1-965016-04-6

This book was professionally typeset on Reedsy.
Find out more at reedsy.com

I

Table of Contents

1

GETTING STARTED

The day before my son was leaving for college, tensions in our house were high. He was packing, saying goodbye to friends – and getting ready to live independently for the first time. He had to fill out paperwork for his college and needed to access his financial aid package on the app. He couldn't find it and kept getting more and more frustrated until he screamed, "I don't know how to do it! You didn't teach me anything! How am I supposed to go to college?"

I was shocked. I thought we had prepared him. He had jobs throughout high school, had his own credit cards, and had savings and investment accounts. We had taught him the value of money and how to budget, and we shared family financial decisions with him.

But now I was panicking. Had I not prepared him well enough? All I could think was, "What else does he need to know?"

I "calmly" told him that he knew more than he thought he did but just to make sure, I would get him a book on financial literacy for young adults. I combed through Amazon, but all the books I found were too long, boring, and general.

I spent the next week typing everything I knew into a Google doc, covering the basics on such things as earnings, investing, saving secrets, and tips on spending well.

A little while later I was talking to a friend who blamed herself because her college-aged son was charging upwards of $150 weekly on delivery apps for snacks and drinks.

I sent her my Google Doc and she loved it. She couldn't believe there was so much useful information in there. Even more shocking, when she gave it to her son he read the whole thing in a day. More friends asked for it, and I kept adding more and more information.

That Google doc served as the outline for this book. I read books, researched, talked to other parents, and advised young people I knew, all to accumulate as much information as I could on early financial decisions. My goal for this book is to give you tips on spending more wisely, saving for the future, and getting the most out of credit cards.

Along the way, you will make mistakes, but this book will save you time and anguish. There's a lot crammed in here, some of which you might already know, some might not fit your life right now. Money is not just the currency of everyday life. If used properly, money can give you freedom.

Freedom to make your own choices and not be dependent on anyone else.

Freedom to marry for love, not necessity.

Freedom to take care of kids or aging parents if you want instead of being locked into a job.

Freedom to live where you want.

Freedom to travel anywhere in the world.

Freedom to live more!

Whatever your situation, spending, and saving will be a part of your life whether it interests you or not. Most every day you will have to make small and large financial choices.

I propose this unusual opinion:

Saving money can be even more fun than spending money.

It's not fun like "go out all night with your friends" kind of fun but saving money feels good because saving on the basics gives you more money to spend on fun things like travel and experiences. I want you to learn to love saving money as much as I do because I think saving is more fun than spending. And, I want to help you be so savvy about spending money that you get double pleasure from it. So that when you do spend money, you will enjoy the purchase itself ALONG with the satisfaction of having been so smart about it.

* * *

Why should you listen to me?

I am not a professional financial advisor. I'm a "regular" person who will lay all of this out for you in easy-to-understand terms. I've packed information to save you thousands of dollars into this little book.

I have been in charge of my financial decisions since I was 16 years old and have been handling money for my family since the day I got engaged to be married. I have made it a lifelong goal to save money and spend wisely, and I am sharing all of my secrets with you.

Even with all my experience, I have made mistakes with money, wasted money, and had many weeks and years when I was BROKE. I used to have to live cheaply and so I got good at it.

I have never seen anyone sharing the practical and **SPECIFIC** ways to do this in any other book. I don't know about you but when I want to learn how to do something, I want to know exactly how. This is why I have crammed this book with practical and specific advice and tips.

If you want to learn **EXACTLY** how to spend less and live better, this book will show you how. Each chapter includes simple actionable strategies that walk you through small steps that will make a big difference in your financial future.

Maybe you are already making a lot of money and think that you don't have to curb your spending. You're wrong. Just because you can afford to waste some money doesn't mean that you should. Having some extra cash allows you to maximize your wealth.

Maybe you are living from paycheck to paycheck, and building a retirement fund seems impossible right now so you think you don't need this book. Wrong again. Starting early sets you up for success later, and learning how to save now will teach you lessons that will pay off in the future.

Whatever your situation, this book will teach you the basics and give you tips to save and spend well. Read this book to learn what kind of strategies make the most sense for you. My goal is to give you the tools to set yourself up for the life you want.

2

THE PSYCHOLOGY OF MONEY

I remember what it's like to be broke. If we were playing the game of one-upping each other on brokenness, I think I could hold my own in most rooms.

I was so broke...

- When I took my used car into the shop to get fixed, I walked eight miles across town down major traffic arteries so that I wouldn't spend money even on bus fare.
- I bought a used rice cooker at a local thrift shop and made a cup of rice every day which was the base of my dinner.
- I flirted with guys I met in bars, not because I had any interest in them, but because I wanted a free drink.
- I drove to Las Vegas for the weekend with a friend with no place to stay and slept in our car.

Okay, when I read that now, it is clear that I took it too far. But the fact is, when I had no money I felt out of control and desperate to cling on to savings.

Money worries caused me a good amount of pain and stress and I would love to help anyone else avert these feelings.

When I was in my early 20s, my girlfriends and I spent many Saturdays shopping. More accurately, my friends would shop and I would hang out with them while they bought designer purses and clothes. I bought very rarely and only pieces from thrift stores or sale sections.

I worked long hours but on a very low salary.. I lived in the smallest cheapest room in our shared apartment, drove my used car sparingly, and saved the maximum allowed to my 401K.

I restricted myself every day. I wouldn't buy anything. I ate basic foods, wore my roommates' clothes, and didn't spend on furniture, entertainment, or anything fun.

It was tough and I often felt deprived. However, it felt good to know that I was doing something that would pay off in the end. Instead of tempting myself shopping, I spent a long time reading catalogs, dog-earing pages, and cutting out photos of looks I liked. I saved every penny from my paychecks.

I worked hard and built a career in marketing. Along the way, I got good at handling money. Finally, I burned out on my career and have all but left the business except for a few consulting opportunities, giving up that income and relearning how to live on less - again. Now, even with minimal employment, I live better than people who I know earned a lot more than me during their careers.

My husband and I own our house, and we have two cars, three pets, a kid in college and one in high school. We live in an expensive neighborhood and have diversified savings that will cover our retirement.

By comparison, a few of our friends who had lucrative careers met with ageism and a shifting economy. Some of these former executives are now in a position where they have to work retail or drive rideshare because they need the money.

These are people whose kids went to fancy private schools and drove expensive cars, but they had debt and little savings. At an age when many people want to work less, they are working more, selling family homes to downsize, and moving to less expensive areas.

A job loss can decimate your income. Unless you're prepared financially, it's very difficult to adjust.

Saving and spending smarter is the base philosophy that helps you prepare yourself for the financial future, whether you keep earning or take financial hits..

While I was forced to live a frugal life, I still had a lot to learn. One time I was out shopping with my friend at the discount store Loehman's. When we went to Loehman's we would always park in the parking garage because they gave you 60 minutes free for shopping. That day, we had been browsing for about 45 minutes so we rushed out of the store to make sure we were able to get out of the parking garage just before the charges started. I raced back to the car and I couldn't find my parking ticket anywhere. I wish I could say that I handled this well, but I didn't. I fell apart. I was so upset that I was going to have to pay the full $14 for a lost parking ticket.

This was a bit of a wake-up call. Money was causing me way too much stress. Would that $14 make an impact on my long-term savings? Probably not but the thought of wasting it was so distressing.

My Loehman's incident wasn't so much about the $14 as it was about responsibility. I felt like a failure because I felt irresponsible. Being responsible makes me feel successful and in control of my life. That meltdown at Loehman's taught me that, while mistakes will happen, being responsible will ultimately define my financial future.

Since that day, I have tried to be responsible with all things financial. I pledged myself that I wouldn't waste money on things that didn't matter and I'd put some larger plans in place to help get me some financial security.

After I calmed down, I decided to understand money better, and understand the power it held over me.

Money issues can play out in many ways. I have a friend who worked as a camera operator and she had a very deep money pattern. Whenever she was working on a movie job, she would spend no money because she was on set long days, eating craft service and coming home exhausted every night. The minute the job was over, she would spend almost all the money she made as fast as she could because she felt so pent up for not spending for weeks on end.

Some other people love to splash their money over others because they love the thrill of the splurge. One friend's husband used to buy dinner and drinks for everyone, every time we went out, no matter the size of the group. He loved spending his money this way. His wife was attracted to this festive spirit when they first met but after they were married and raising children, she asked him to cut back on treating everyone all the time. It was very difficult for him because it was part of his identity. They clashed over whether it was more important to treat others or save their money for their family.

There are many different ways to save and splurge and it is a very individual choice. You get to decide when you think it's okay to indulge and when it's best to spend smart. If you are in a relationship with combined finances like the couple I mentioned above, it's best to discuss spending with your partner so you understand the plan and can come up with spending strategies that make you both comfortable.

How you choose to spend your money is a very personal thing. Understanding what's important to you will help you adopt successful strategies for your finances.

* * *

Here are some initial questions about spending that may get you started thinking about how you want to live financially.

What are your top priorities for your life?

Do you want a beautiful home filled with nice things?

Is having a prestigious career an important ambition?

Do you want to retire early or work for yourself?

Do you want to travel and experience as much of the world as you can?

Do you want to be healthy- sleep well and be able to take care of yourself?

Do you hope to leave a legacy for your family?

Do you want to contribute to the world? Live in abundance so that you can share your riches with those around you who aren't so fortunate.

Do you want to give to causes that are important to you, and volunteer your time in service of others?

Think about a time you made a mistake with money. How did that make you feel?

When my kids played AYSO soccer, the coaches told them that there were only winners and learners. Think of a time when you made a mistake – buying something you didn't need, overspending, etc. Did you bury your head in the sand and forget it? Or did you take a step back and try to understand where you made your mistake? Thinking back to that time, what did you learn? Were you upset because of the loss of money or because of what it represented to you?

Microsoft Co-Founder Bill Gates, in his first 10 years as a billionaire, still flew economy class. He probably flew first class once and realized that the warm hand towel, meal, and extra legroom weren't worth the extra $1000 the first-class ticket cost. To him, first class wasn't glamorous and didn't make him feel important – to him it was a waste of money. Knowing the value of something and its worth to you is everything.

Think about a time when spending money made you happy.

Understanding exactly what makes you happy will help you understand your financial priorities. I can think of many times when spending money, even outside of my budget, was worth it. According to a 2012 study published in "The Journal of Positive Psychology," people are happier when they spend money on experiences rather than things. I completely agree. My best memories of dropping large amounts of money were with friends and family doing something fun like riding a snowmobile in Iceland, taking a surf lesson, and having great seats for my favorite band.

It took me a long time to have perspective and learn what brings happiness to me and what doesn't. My daughter in New York recently bought a ticket to a "Santa Con" where you dress up like Santa and barhop. She went and didn't like it. She wasn't into the Santa thing or the day drinking. However, she did feel good because the entrance fees go to a charity. She learned not to waste money on pub crawls, but she also learned that she takes pleasure in donating money to causes she believes in.

How do you spend? Are you compulsive or reserved?

You won't be shocked that I'll argue for thought-out and strategic spending. However, I understand that some people enjoy compulsive spending. Gambling is a great example that gives people a huge thrill, despite the likelihood of losing. Charitable auctions are also events where you will probably overspend but you might derive more pleasure from "winning" than you do from the item itself. If that "bingo" moment is worth the hit in your pocketbook, that is very important to know. Then you will be able to set limits on how much you gamble or spend before you get into the heat of the moment. Think about how you feel as you spend. Does it give you a rush? Do you do it for the thrill but then feel regret?

Are you frugal or do you spend money freely?

How do you feel about treating others?

How do you feel when someone treats you?

Do you feel like you deserve it?

If you come from a wealthy family, do you have guilt about that, or do you have doubts about being able to maintain that same lifestyle?

Maybe you grew up in a wealthy family and you have insecurities that you were "handed" a head start. Try to re-frame that. Many squander an inheritance. It is a challenge to manage money especially if you are given it when you are young. If you are handling large amounts of money, it is important to learn more about spending money to use it wisely and responsibly.

Do you have issues with spending because you grew up in a family where money was tight?"

Many people who come from humble beginnings have issues with money - both with impetuous overspending and not knowing how to save. My husband grew up in a family that for many years struggled with money. He still has anxiety about wanting to overspend on things like buying presents for our kids because he wanted more as a child. But he also has issues saving, as counter-intuitive as it may seem, because he worries about seeming cheap by using coupons or asking for a better deal. Understanding financial triggers like these will help you overcome them.

3

SAVING

"Do not save what is left after spending, but spend what is left after saving". –
Warren Buffett

As a teenager, I learned some basic principles about money from my father. The first thing he taught me is that if you get an 8% rate of return, your money will double in about 7 years. Simple, and I never forget it. That image of doubling was powerful. He also told me his favorite words: compound interest.

Compound interest is the interest on savings calculated on both the initial principal and the accumulated interest from previous periods. "Interest on interest," or the power of compound interest, will make a sum grow faster than simple interest, which is calculated only on the principal amount. Compounding multiplies money at an accelerated rate. The greater the number of compounding periods, the greater the compound interest will be.

For example, putting $10 away now into an investment account would amount to $68 in twenty-five years (if we assume an 8% interest rate). That may not sound impressive but when you think that $10,000 would be $68,485, you start to see why it is so powerful. On the other hand, if you wait and don't start saving until 15 years later, that same $10,000 will only grow to $14,693.

Time is your greatest asset. The younger you start saving, the more your money will grow.

To Budget Or Not Budget

I'll admit that I have never been able to stick to a budget because I have always found budgets boring and time-consuming. I would rather keep a general understanding of my budget in my head without constantly checking the numbers. Sure, I get things wrong sometimes, but I'm never too far over or below where I think my spending is.

If you are doing ok paying your bills every month and having enough left over to spend on needs, wants, and savings, great. Don't let anyone bully you into thinking you must make a budget.

If you have chronic issues with overspending, following a strict budget is a good way to keep yourself in line.

* * *

When considering how to budget, think about these three things

1. **Do you have the potential to spend more than you can cover?** First and foremost, set up automatic payments for credit cards, rent/mortgage, utilities, etc.Also, make sure you have safeguards in place so you never bounce a payment, as that could cost you fees and time spent fixing issues with your account.
2. **Pay yourself first.** I sound like a broken record, "save, save, save." But, you will thank yourself if you put money aside for savings before you do anything else. That's the best way to make sure that

you are making progress towards your saving goals. This means that you take a percentage or a predetermined amount out of every paycheck and put it towards your savings or investing bucket. By "paying yourself first" you are making sure that you won't blow the entire amount and have nothing for your future. If you are saving money regularly, then following a strict budget becomes less of a worry because you will have broken out of the living paycheck to paycheck cycle.

3. **Spend mindfully.** As long as you are spending on experiences and goods that bring you joy, comfort, or whatever else is important to you, then you are spending your money wisely.

To cover the first item on the list, you first need to look at what you are earning and how much it costs to cover your musts: housing, utilities, insurance, and a small emergency fund. Once you subtract all those fixed costs you will have an idea of your disposable income. From that, **decide how much you can afford to put into a savings or investment account.**

If you think things are tight, start with a goal that makes sense to you, ideally a nice round number around 10%. I like to set up an automatic withdrawal that will pull a certain amount of money from the checking account every week. Do this for at least two months. If it's going well and you find that you have money left over, increase the savings to 15%. If that goes well, take it to 20%, and so on. If you find that you are cutting it too close every month, dial it back to for a while. Any savings is a win.

If you feel like your money is disappearing every month and you are struggling to remember where it went, one thing that is helpful for mindful spending is going to surprise and even shock people because some financial gurus will tell you to cut them up: credit cards!

4

CREDIT CARDS

As much as I love credit cards now, they were not always my friends. I got my first credit card when I was 16. I felt so grown up and used it every chance I could. I can remember one thing I bought with it during that first month —probably things like earrings and lip gloss. It was all very exciting, until of course the first statement showed up. Somehow I managed to run up a bill of $300. This was when $300 was a lot of money and, of course, I couldn't even come close to paying off the balance. I felt sick for days, worrying about what I was going to do.

Finally, I went to my mother in tears. She said that she would pay it off but if it happened again, I would have to work it off doing household chores at $1/hour. This was crazy low, but she made the point that spending has consequences.

I never did it again.

Carrying credit card debt is one of the worst financial situations you can experience but it is, unfortunately, very common. Current statistics show that 61% of Americans are in credit card debt with an average balance of just over $5K. Paying 20% interest is like borrowing money from the mob in a 1940s movie - they'll keep taking more, and you'll get further in the hole.

If you ever get into trouble with a credit card, don't feel bad about it. The important thing is to be open when you get into trouble because it's easier to fix it when it's a small balance rather than when it grows bigger and worse. This is the opposite of compound interest — where the debt keeps growing off of itself.

My roommate got into a similar predicament when she amassed $22,000 in credit card debt. She finally told me about it, and it made me crazy that she would be paying 20% annual interest to Visa. I offered to pay it off for her, and we set up a repayment plan where she paid me back at a much better rate. After that, she also says that she has never had debt again.

If you do get into debt, don't be too hard on yourself but don't put your head in the sand. Be honest about it so that you can find the best solution. Friends and family are the best people to help in the short term if that is an option. If they can loan you the money, it is best to draw up an agreement about how you plan to repay them, with or without interest.

However, if you have credit card debt, many times your family won't have the means or inclination to help you.

The most important thing about having debt is to deal with it. Controlling and paying off this debt must be a top spending priority. Here are a few ways to do this:

1. Open a new credit card where you can transfer the balance. This sounds counter-intuitive that instead of telling you to pay off your debt, I'm suggesting you keep it. However, cards often have introductory rates at 0.0% for several months. If you could transfer your balance to one of those low rates, it would buy you time. You will still need to keep paying down your balance monthly but at least you won't be adding to that balance as you pay it down. To

do this, you will need a good (likely above 670) **FICO score**. If you don't have that, keep reading for other options. ***FICO Score**- a three-digit number that lenders use to predict how likely a person is to repay a loan on time.

2. Get a personal loan- Websites like Nerdwallet.com have information on personal loans. Even if the rates aren't super low they will be less than rates charged by the big cards.
3. As a last resort if you are reading this and you are already in a significant amount of debt you may want to look into a debt settlement company like Nationaldebtrelief.com. This is a company that will offer you one or two possible paths:

Debt settlement:

Debt relief companies like Freedom and Accredited will negotiate with your credit card company so you will pay less than you owe. The creditor will pay off the remaining debt and set you up on a payment plan often at a reduced interest rate.

Debt consolidation:

These companies combine your debt into one loan with a single payment often at a reduced interest rate. This is similar to getting a personal loan and should only be explored if you cannot get it on your own.

You can also negotiate directly with the credit card company yourself. If you explain that you are going to be unable to pay off your debt, they will most likely set you up on a payment plan and lower the interest rate. Just know that they will no longer allow you to use your card and this will negatively impact your credit.

Any of these tactics can negatively impact your credit score but don't get bogged down by worrying about your credit score that you are stuck not doing anything. Credit scores are important but there are ways to repair them, and it's most important to get out of debt.

A credit score is just a prediction of your credit behavior, such as how likely you are to pay a loan back on time, based on information from your credit reports. It will go down if you miss payments, carry a high debt balance, or have access to too much credit but with regular, on-time payments and lower balances, it will slowly go up.

After I got out of trouble, I learned to take advantage of credit cards.

Some books suggest putting cash in labeled envelopes and only using that money for certain expenses, such as utilities, etc. If you have a spending problem and you have gone into debt multiple times, that may be the system for you. However, if you know how or can learn to use credit cards, instead of them using you, then they can be excellent financial resources with great benefits.

Most credit cards let you earn loyalty points. Points are accumulated per dollar spent and loyalty points can be exchanged for free travel, such as rental cars, hotels, flights, and more. They can also be traded in for cash and used to pay off your bill or for merchandise, although those redemptions are not nearly as valuable.

In addition to all the freebies, credit cards come with purchase protections, advocate for you if someone charges you incorrectly, offer free car rental insurance and other coverage, and provide annual spending reports that break down how you spent over the last year. If you understand their rules and offers, you can game the system so that their benefits far exceed the risks.

Here are some key points to credit cards:

1. Make sure this is the right time in your life to open a credit card. Every credit card you open negatively impacts your credit (FICO) score. If you need to keep your score high because you are about to buy or rent a house for example, you may need to wait. If you don't

have a high income or long credit history, your purchasing power is limited, so you need to use your credit wisely.

2. Pick the right credit card- The more expensive cards (cards with higher fees and minimums) have better purchase and travel protections. However, depending upon your spending habits, a low or no-fee card may be the best choice for you. As a general rule, skip the store credit cards (like a Best Buy or Marriott credit card) and start your credit card journey with a low-cost or free credit card that has a healthy sign-up bonus (which can come as a chunk of points, travel insurance, and/or purchase protections). At the time of publication and for the past few years, the American Express Green card or the Chase Sapphire Preferred have been the two best beginner cards.These are both low-cost cards that have sign-up bonuses as high as a 75,000 point grant after you spend 3K in the first six months. This boost will help you have a stash of points right away.
3. Once you start moving up in income brackets, you can start considering the next tier of cards. To find your best card match, check Nerdwallet. Pick a card with the best sign-up bonus.
4. Try to use your credit card for everything, unless it is for something where using a credit card charges you a fee (like property taxes). If you are out to dinner with friends, offer to use your credit card to pay and have your friends Venmo/Zelle you back. By taking the charge, you get all of the points for the entire meal, not just your portion.
5. Always avoid carrying any amount of debt. Set your credit card on autopay and pay off the entire balance every month. The only exception to this rule is if you get a new credit card — sometimes there is an introductory 0% rate. If that is the case, you can run up charges on the credit card until the rate changes. This is an advanced technique for juggling credit card debt that I would not

suggest you try unless you are sure you can track and manage it.

6. Pick a card with a sign-up bonus that you will be able to fulfill. For example, Sapphire Preferred often has a sign-up deal where you get 60,000 points if you spend $4,000 in the first three months. There's no point in a huge sign-up bonus if you aren't going to hit the minimum spend. My college-aged daughter recently signed up for a new credit card because of the great introductory offer and was able to get a free flight to Costa Rica for spring break. But I had to keep on top of her and I even bought several items for myself using her card so that she'd meet the minimum. If you aren't willing to pay this close attention to hitting the requirement, then don't bother.
7. Read your terms of service and know what the credit cards cover and don't. Many cards include roadside assistance, rental car insurance and travel cancellation insurance. Before you travel, read or call the card and double-check if it covers you. If they do, you will possibly save hundreds of dollars not needing to buy rental car insurance or travel insurance.
8. Check your statements regularly for fraud. This happens more often than you think. If you see any charges you do not recognize, contact your credit card immediately. Sometimes thieves charge very small amounts to test if a card has been reported and then charge a big amount, so be sure to check all the charges frequently.
9. Checking your statements regularly is the best way to catch those recurring charges and make sure you still want them. If you see a Spotify charge and realize you haven't used Spotify in a month, it gives you a minute to think about if you still want it. This especially is true for fitness/health club charges. There is an App called **Rocket Money** that will search for all of your subscriptions and even cancel them for you if you want. There is a free version and if you feel like you don't have a handle on these, it could be worth getting the app

and running a check. I found the app to be extra work so I ended up deleting it, but it could work for you.

10. Don't be afraid to file a dispute if you have an issue with a merchant. Thankfully, most cards make this very easy to do. Usually, all you have to do is click on the charge in question and it will take you to something that says "Is there a problem" or something along those lines. Whatever the problem, select that. Most cards will grant you a "conditional credit" while they investigate the matter. On their back end, they contact the merchant and then will recharge you if they agree with the merchant or make the credit permanent if they side with you. They will always ask if you have tried to remedy the problem with the merchant, so try that first. If you are unhappy with a service or purchase, always try to solve it with the merchant directly. You will be surprised how often good businesses will go out of their way to make customers happy. If they do not, then the credit card is the best one to help. Recently I got a shipment that was marked as delivered but I never got the package. Even though the merchant insisted it was delivered and would not give me credit, the credit card company refunded me the $110 for the tennis shoes that never arrived.
11. When you go over your monthly statement, take a minute to go through and remember each charge. If you see the bill for a dinner, remember who you were with, and if it was worth the expense. If it was something you bought, think about it you are happy or regretful about the purchase.
12. Ignore the card's spending limit. This is set by the credit card and has nothing to do with your budget. If you regularly pay your full balance on time, your card will often raise your spending limit and announce it to you like it's some big reward. This is the same as a Las Vegas casino inviting you to a no-limit VIP table. Follow your budget, not theirs. Decide you are spending $500/month or

whatever you can afford and stick to it. Check your spending once a week to make sure you are on track. If you are running high, figure out what you are doing to curtail it. It's always easiest to self-correct on the fly.

5

COOKING AT HOME

The first spending category to master is Food and Drink because it's relatively low dollar so any mistakes won't be that expensive. However, it's a great category to see some immediate results. It is also the issue that will arise most often in your life.

Although everyone needs to eat, people value food differently. Some people don't care about food. My husband has this one friend they call the robot because they never see him eat or drink anything. Of course, he eats but he doesn't care much about it. My sister said once that if she could take a pill and never have to eat again, she would.

Most people, however, love food, which means they're going to be buying, ordering, or preparing approximately 20 meals a week. That's 1000 meals a year! If you went out to eat or ordered DoorDash for every meal, you'd spend tens of thousands of dollars on dining alone. This is not financially sustainable for most people and a huge waste of money. You need to find a balance that makes sense for your lifestyle.

Food Hit List:

If you want to be successful at enjoying eating at home and saving thousands of dollars a year, it is helpful to have a kitchen stocked with inexpensive, healthy foods on permanent rotation. There are lots of fill-ins but if you have these ten things, you will never starve.

1. Bananas- usually about 25 cents each, clean, portable, healthy.
2. Oats- serve them hot in the winter with nuts or berries, and turn them into granola in the summer.
3. Rice- buy a rice cooker if you don't have one already. They will run you for less than $25 at Facebook Marketplace, Goodwill, or Amazon. Buy the big bags of rice at the Asian markets. Brown rice is healthier, but if you don't eat it, basmati and white rice are still great staples.
4. Eggs - cheap easy protein- for fried rice, omelets, salads, etc. They are one of the most important foods for living well on a budget because they are perfect in many situations. My husband and I say, "Put an egg on it," because you can put a fried fried egg atop almost everything and it works.
5. Pasta-versatile. I like to keep rice noodles on hand along with traditional Italian noodles.
6. Canned beans- Garbanzo, black, re-fried, kidney covers most recipes - store well and are a cheap, high fiber protein.
7. Canned tomato paste- the base for pasta sauce, chili, and pizzas. It is smaller than jars of sauce and doesn't have sugar added. You can customize it to how you like your tomato and it tastes brighter and more like real tomatoes.
8. Potatoes- Consider Sweet potatoes or yams for more vitamins but it's hard to beat the flavor and versatility of russets and Yukon golds.
9. Quinoa- higher protein than rice and cooks more quickly.
10. Freezer food- frozen protein, vegetables, fruit, and pizza crusts so you always have something to make and aren't tempted to order food.

You may notice this is missing fruits and vegetables. Although they are great nutritionally, they should be bought more sparingly. Fresh produce can go bad quickly, so think of fruits and vegetables as a frequent purchase, not a bulk purchase.

Grocery Shopping Rules:

You will need to grocery shop your whole life so you may as well learn how to be a smart shopper. Grocery stores are very competitive and want your loyalty so the stores make it easy to save.

1. You don't have to shop with a list, but it is helpful to have at least a general plan and get in and out of the store without wandering the aisles so you aren't tempted by the items you don't need. Personally, I don't like to write out a shopping list. Instead, I look at the app for the grocery stores I'm considering (Whole Foods, Ralph's, Vons, Safeway, etc.) before I go to see what is on sale. That way I have a plan before I walk through the door. Wandering will get you in trouble.
2. It sounds obvious but most store stickers or Amazon listings have a per-unit price which makes it easy to comparison shop.
3. Don't (always) be a brand snob. Many generic or store brands are the same, so always consider them. However, if there is a brand that you really think is better, buy that. For example, we usually buy store-brand shredded cheeses, but I've learned that Philadelphia cream cheese really is the best cream cheese and I'd rather pay a little more for that than eat the store-brand. Same with English muffins. Thomas' cost more but in my mind are worth it. In short, keep an open mind for the generics but go for a brand name if you think the quality is worth it.
4. If you have Amazon Prime, use the Whole Foods app. They have very aggressive deals for Prime Members so I recommend shopping

their weekly sales. Not only does this save you money, but it is often a rotation that can be used for automatic meal planning.

5. Pavillions/Vons, Ralphs, Albertsons, Bristol/Gelsons, or whatever regional major grocery store chain is in your area: look at their sales fliers. Most have weekly sales with greatly reduced prices. Many have loyalty points and rewards. It is easy to sign up and it will often save you considerable money.
6. Know where to shop. If I'm deciding what to make for dinner, I'll check the apps for Vons, Whole Foods, Gelson's, etc., and check their sales items. This gives me a natural rotation of different foods as well as saving money. Saving on the majority of food makes it easier to splurge on special items that aren't available at the same quality at the major stores. For bagels, I frequent a real NY bagel store which is more expensive but a much superior bagel. I also know that the local Persian market always has the best deals on produce so I will buy a ton of vegetables there and splurge on their homemade dips and marinated meats.
7. Just like with fruits and vegetables, be mindful when buying in bulk. Don't be lured into bulk purchases by lower prices, only to end up having too much food than you can eat. A co-worker of mine once found a great deal on a 20-pound box of carrots. He loved carrots but after the first 2 pounds, he never wanted to see another one again. Want to go to Costco or buy in bulk? See if you can split a membership with roommates or friends. You split the cost of the membership and large amounts of food that are often too much for a couple or single person to eat before it spoils.
8. Are you traveling?- It usually saves money to stay at an AirBnB or VRBO as you have a kitchen for taking some meals at your lodging. However, whenever we stay at a vacation rental, I'm shocked by how much food the previous travelers have left behind. If practical, take a look at your temporary kitchen to know what you have before

you go to the store. Staples like oil, spices, and condiments add up and often they are already there. If you need to shop, only buy what you will use. This is not the time to try the most complicated recipes with a long list of ingredients. Try to stick with meals where you know you will use the supplies. Spaghetti bolognese is a good dinner because it's sauce, meat and pasta. Egg in a hole is the best vacation breakfast because you only need eggs, a loaf of bread, and butter.

9. If you are trying to eat healthy, you need to focus on less expensive but versatile protein sources. One way to do this is to embrace frozen protein- I used to think that frozen fish, meat, and chicken were inferior but in reality, most of the meat and seafood that is sold in the grocery store was defrosted. Buying it frozen is one level fresher so you can decide exactly when to defrost. Buying frozen fruits and vegetables works for some situations. Frozen berries work well in oatmeal, and frozen vegetables are perfect for stir fries and one-pot meals.

My kids have been grocery shopping since they were old enough to walk in a store alone. Now that my child is at college in a dorm with a kitchen, her savvy shopping has come in handy. She found a great Asian Market in Chinatown where she could get 50 frozen dumplings for $20. She started having dumpling parties and inviting friends over. They bring the sides and the drinks and she provides the dumplings. Not only has that resulted in many fun nights but also, but they also reciprocate and she has noticed she has gotten more invitations since she started hosting dumpling nights.

Special Note about Coffee:

Financial Planners vehemently preach against coffee stores. Some like Suze Orman say they would never pay for fancy coffee ("for the price of a cup of coffee…"). Others say that it's not a focus and isn't going to change the trajectory of your financial health so why not buy coffee? I have a history with coffee. When I was starting out as an assistant, I used to buy coffee at least once a day. I went to work early and stayed late, so it was a survival instinct. However, it was excessive. A generous co-worker once gave me a $500 Starbucks gift card for my birthday, and I was shocked when I used it up in only a couple of months. That made me realize how much I was spending on coffee, and I stopped buying it for a long time. Instead, I drank the (not very good but free) coffee at the office.

When I had a baby, I stayed home with my infant and I started going out to coffee again. I was so tired, and we needed a reason to get out of the house. We'd go to our corner Starbucks and my son loved to look out for big trucks, so we called this activity "Starbucks and Trucks." Sometimes we would go alone, sometimes we'd meet a friend. I considered this a worthwhile expense because I got hours of entertainment for my son and myself for the price of a small drip coffee.

A good Starbucks cheat is that coffee and iced tea come with free refills. I often get a coffee or iced tea, enjoy it at a table, then get a refill and take it to go.

If it's at a time in your life when your going-out-to-coffee habits are giving you something rewarding, stick with it. You might have a group you see regularly at your local coffee shop, you might have a crush you see in line a lot, or you might like to use the WiFi for a few hours. However, if you are just picking up a coffee on the way to work, then I do agree with experts who advise against wasting money on coffee.

If you're getting Starbucks every day, you're likely spending upwards of $2000 per year, which I'd prefer you put into savings or use on a bigger, more noticeable splurge. However, that doesn't mean that I'm saying to NEVER do it. Splurge once in a while if it's an activity to see a friend. And, always be sure to get the free coffee on your birthday (download the Starbucks app and input your birthday). Pick the most outrageous Venti (XL) drink on the menu to try it.

Most businesses offer free coffee, so if you are working in an office and it's drinkable, by all means, take advantage of that. It's usually not the best coffee in the world but it's hot and it's free and you could always treat yourself to some Torani syrup or your preferred cream/milk or milk alternative.

If you are traveling, know that there is free morning coffee in most hotel lobbies. Look out for that and ask about it when you check in because they often don't mention it up front.

Another idea for travel depending on where you will be is that it can be a good idea to bring a package of those little Starbucks instant coffee packets. One of those stirred into boiling water makes a surprisingly decent cup of coffee for less than a dollar.

6

RESTAURANTS

The restaurant industry would like you to believe since most people enjoy spending money on experiences rather than things, it is worth spending money to eat at restaurants. That may be, but think about what you are paying for when you go to a restaurant- is it an experience or the food?

Dining at restaurants is almost always much more expensive than dining at home. You're paying for the service, the atmosphere, the ambiance.

If you are trying to save money, plan to prepare the majority of your meals yourself versus getting them at restaurants. The more you cook, the better you will get at it. Most likely, you will enjoy it more and eat well at home. Almost any dish can be recreated at home for a fraction of the cost of what it would be in a restaurant. Once you are comfortable in the kitchen, you can purchase expensive ingredients to recreate "treat" meals for a fraction of the price. For example, my family loves to get lobster rolls as an indulgence. These are typically $25+ each at most restaurants and usually are small portioned. I recently noticed lobster meat on sale for $40/pound at our local seafood market. While that sounds very expensive and way more than I would normally recommend paying per pound of meat, we were able to make four rolls out of that pound of lobster meat. The lobster meat, some nice brioche hot dog buns, and some butter cost us less than $50, and the rolls were overstuffed compared to what we'd get at a restaurant for $100.

If you are eating a lot of restaurant meals, it's helpful to think about why you want to go. Which one of these sounds like you?

The Too Tired Diner:

A lot of people end up grabbing food from a restaurant because they are working a lot and are too tired to make something at home. Restaurants love take-out and delivery because they're charging the same amount without using any space in the dining room or taxing the wait staff.

The most efficient way to snap out of this cycle is meal prep. Meal prep sounds like a lot of work but isn't. Spending a little bit of time to prepare healthy foods on the weekends is one way to save time and money during the week. Chicken breast and ground turkey are good proteins that you make in batches and are versatile for use in several different dishes.

Another option is to join one of the food delivery services like Everyplate, Hello Fresh, Factor, GreenChef, and BlueApron. Some of them are fairly reasonable, likely cheaper than dining out and many offer very generous discounts for the first trial. So, every time you know you are having a big week coming up and won't be able to cook, treat yourself to trying a new service. Just be sure to cancel at the end of the reduced-price trial unless you love it and decide it's worth it for you.

The Bored Diner:

You don't mind cooking but you can't think of anything to make. This is one time when scrolling through social media might save you money. There are tons of Instagram reels featuring yummy recipes for inspiration. Or, are you tired of sitting at the same table? Mix it up. Can you organize a lunch with friends somewhere outside, in a yard or courtyard, or bring food to the beach or park? If you are eating at home, make it special by inviting over a friend. Add candles and play thematic music at dinner. If you are hosting a date, remember that it's more fun and personal to cook for someone instead of dropping $200 at a fancy restaurant.

The Adventurous Diner:

Maybe you're foodie who pays attention to the newest eateries, or maybe you have your bucket list of restaurants. If so, maintaining healthy finances is the best way to fund these splurges. Perhaps you wouldn't mind cooking but your cooking skill is not up to the level where you can make all the types of dishes you want to eat. In this case, think about becoming a better cook. You will never regret this as preparing food is something you will do for the rest of your life. Some countless websites and videos will help you on your journey. Taking a cooking class is a fun night out with a friend or S.O., or even a first date.

While you are on the path to mastering these more sophisticated dishes, make sure that when you go out, you are going somewhere where you are getting the things that are not easily recreated at home, whatever that means to you.

Here are a few occasions where it may be tempting to go out:

Sushi- A home sushi night is fun but if you want a special experience with more kinds of fish and the artistry involved in some Japanese dishes, it's hard to replicate that at home and likely worth it to go out for it once in a while.

Benihana, Medieval Times, or "experience restaurants" - These can be worth it for the experience once in a while if that's fun for you. Weeknight prices are often lower than weekends. Look for coupons, promos, etc.

Brunch- Usually a big money maker for the restaurant. The unlimited mimosas are cheap prosecco and cheap orange juice. Try to host a brunch at your home or a local park instead. Have everyone bring something.

Happy Hour- You may think it is for seniors who want to eat at 4 pm but if you learn to embrace happy hours you can find some bargains that give you all of the experience of eating out - no dishes, full service, etc. without the full cost. One caveat- be sure you know what you are getting. Sometimes places are just offering half portions for half the price. That's fine if you know and you want to try a place without spending a lot of money but you may not be getting extra value. Don't be afraid to ask the waiter if something is a smaller portion than the usual. I especially recommend happy hour for trying out a new restaurant. It is a way to get a drink and try a few dishes at a discount to see if you like the food and service before you commit. Often the hours are early but some places do a reverse happy hour where the discount runs from 9-11 pm or they do Taco Tuesdays where they have discounted specials all night long. A deal that the restaurant promotes is likely to be better because they know it will be many people's first introduction to a place so they usually do a good job making it worthwhile. It is easy to search on Yelp for Happy Hours or Google in your city for lists. Also, follow restaurants you like on social media so you know when they advertise promotions.

Restaurant Weeks:

Most big cities have regularly scheduled "Restaurant Weeks." During these weeks, restaurants present special menus. They usually include a free dessert or appetizer but some of them are more generous, especially for newer restaurants. Check if your city hosts a restaurant week and get on their email list.

Credit Card Promotions:

These are often targeted promotions with cash back at certain restaurants. Make sure you are signed up for alerts for promotions from your credit card to take advantage of these. Visa once offered a promotional meal at a high-end Mexican restaurant nearby. I signed up for a modest price. My husband was able to take a friend and enjoy a 4-course meal with an introduction from the chef.

Bars/Clubbing:

If you are going out for a night of clubbing or bar hopping, consider meeting up to get ready or pregame at someone's first. It's fun to prep for the night as a group and then you save on drinks if you have a drink or two at home. When you get to the club, alternate water and drinks. You will drink less, feel better the next day, and save money.

Group Dinners:

Try to know the plan ahead of time. Is it a work dinner? Great, then hopefully the company is picking up the tab. I wouldn't recommend ordering the shaved truffles or lobster but maybe order a protein entree over the pizza or pasta or something that you are more likely to make/order cheaply on your own. Is it a friend's birthday dinner? In that case, buy your dinner and split the cost of the birthday honoree. If you eat and drink in line with the group, expect an even split. If you opt to get extra, it is polite to offer to pay more. And, though it sounds counter-intuitive, even if you don't drink or choose a less expensive dish, don't count on paying less. You can try to ask the server for a separate check, but not all restaurants will allow that. If you are stuck in a group meal that will be an even split, try to order last. If most people are ordering surf and turf, then you may want to choose a high-dollar entree, too. At least you won't be resentful for paying more than what you ordered.

Tipping:

When you are feeling broke, it can be tempting to try to save on the tip.

If it's one of those iPads with add 22 percent, 25, or 30, feel free to click on "other amount" and add 15 percent if the service was only satisfactory. If you aren't sure, ask the staff if they get the tips. Remember to tip more generously on lower-priced food. For counter service, it's OK to skip the tip unless they go out of their way to be nice or give you something special. My rule of thumb: if I order standing up, no tip.

Restaurant Gift Cards:

Restaurants often give generous discounts on gift cards, especially around the holidays. Take advantage of these if you like the restaurant and will go but be very careful of expiration dates. There are also national groups like InKind that offer heavily discounted deals.

Groupon, Living Social, etc.:

I've found that these are just a bummer. The best offers are usually for restaurants in trouble, and it feels like the restaurants aren't that excited about honoring these deals. I've used these in the past, I have to say it's usually not worth it, especially if it's a special occasion or date.

Too Good to Go:

This is an app with heavily discounted food, mainly breads and such that need to be sold on the day they are made. My daughter started doing this in Manhattan. She's getting weekly bagels from the hottest bagel places and having people over on Sundays. Since she's bought the bagels, people bring lox, prosecco, etc. It has limited availability so I hope they thrive and keep expanding. If Too Good to Go is not in your area yet, keep an eye out.

InKind:

This is a network of more than 1250 restaurants ranging from coffee shops to Michelin star level across the country. They offer generous promotional credits when you purchase meals or gift cards within their network. https://inkind.com/#explore-restaurants

Yelp Elite:

If you like dining out and you enjoy posting about your experiences, you may want to pursue becoming a Yelp Elite. By being certified as an Elite, you get invited to special promotional restaurant events. My daughter recently got Elite status in New York and has been invited to multiple restaurants for special discounted and free dining events.

7

SHOPPING

A Harvard Professor was recently quoted as saying that 95 % of purchasing decisions are subconscious and driven by emotion, not logic. We may think we are deciding to buy, but we are just pawns!

Before you buy, think WHY you are buying and if you should be buying at all.

Shopping can trigger a dopamine response in the brain. Dopamine is a neurotransmitter associated with the brain's reward system, and it plays a crucial role in the motivation and reinforcement of rewarding behaviors. When we engage in activities that are pleasurable or satisfying, such as making a purchase, our brains may release dopamine, contributing to feelings of pleasure and reward.

The process of shopping, especially when it involves finding and acquiring something you desire, can be associated with positive emotions. The anticipation of buying a desired item, the act of making a purchase, and the ownership of the new possession can all contribute to the release of dopamine. This is often referred to as the "shopping high" or the positive emotional experience associated with acquiring something novel or desirable.

However, while shopping can provide a temporary boost in mood through dopamine release, relying on shopping as a source of happiness or a coping mechanism can lead to unhealthy patterns, including overspending and financial stress. The positive effects of the dopamine response from shopping are short-lived, and they will do very little to address underlying emotional or psychological needs.

People vary in their susceptibility to the dopamine response triggered by shopping. Personal values, financial situation, and emotional well-being can influence the impact of shopping on an individual so be mindful of your shopping habits. If they are causing distress or financial difficulties, you want to explore healthier coping mechanisms and seek support if needed.

For example, maybe you have had a terrible week. The weekend is coming and you are feeling low. You may have heard the phrase "retail therapy." This was coined because people do soothe themselves with shopping and you may be tempted to buy something to get that dopamine hit.

What can you do instead?

1. Browse. Some people might tell you not to even look if you cannot afford to shop. I find the opposite is true. It doesn't cost anything to look so look as inspiration, and also as a way of getting over it. I like to go to the fanciest stores that are so out of reach that I won't even be tempted to purchase. One of my favorite places to go is the top floor of the ultra-fancy Bergdorf Goodman in New York. They have a beautiful home wares department and a spectacular collection of Christmas decor. The tree skirts are bejeweled and cost thousands of dollars. I'm never going to buy one of them but the act of browsing and looking at all of the beautiful things satisfies that part of me that wants to shop.
2. Put it in your cart. For internet shopping, sometimes you may want

to put that item in your cart. This may trigger a feeling of relief because you know that it is there if you want it. If you then step away, you may find you don't need to go back to it.

3. Go for a walk or do something active to get a hit of dopamine from exercise.
4. Look at your goal sheet or balance sheet. Focusing on a positive achievement, however small, can also give you that positive feeling.
5. Look at the reason you are saving. Keep a photo of the trip or couch or whatever is the object of your longer-term savings goal. Looking at it can help keep you on track.
6. Instead of buying, sell something. Maybe you have something that has been sitting around for a long time and this is a good moment to list it for sale.
7. Buy something tiny. Sometimes nothing will work and you want to buy something but you shouldn't. Buy something useful but low cost. If buying a piece of clothing or makeup for less than $10 on Amazon will give you that shopping satisfaction, then doing that once in a while won't completely bust your budget and may allow you to go back to a saving mindset.
8. Get goods for free. Join BuyNothing groups where people give things away. Think of organizing a swap with friends for either temporary or permanent swaps. Sometimes you aren't ready to get rid of a piece but won't wear it for a while. This works especially well with roommates. Just be sure to care for their goods better or as well as your own. Also, don't swap easy-to-lose items like gloves, scarves, and coats which can be left behind. I also don't recommend swapping expensive or sentimental jewelry or pieces that could be easily stained (think white shirts and sweaters).

Doing one of these options will still give you that dopamine hit you are craving but won't hurt your budget.

OK, obviously not shopping is for emotional reasons. What if you actually need something? For example, your athletic shoes are worn out. How can you make your spending go the farthest?

Maximizing your purchasing power:

Generally, if you are in the market to buy something, don't buy it the first time unless it's a limited-time offer. It's best to fully investigate all of the options before you purchase so you don't find something better later and have buyer's remorse. If my husband needs new running shoes, he used to go to a sports store or to the ASICS website without any further thought. Now he tells me what he wants. I'm almost always able to find the exact item for 10% or more off.

There are many browser extensions for making purchases. Ignore them. The only one you need is Rakuten. Once you've added Rakuten to your browser (preferably Chrome), start any shopping trips through their site so you earn cash back or points if you link an American Express Card. The points accumulate with each purchase, and you can transfer those points to numerous airline and hotel partners.

Here are some of my favorite tricks for getting the best deals online:

#1: Move your cursor near the "back" arrow on the browser. This is called "exit intent," and the websites are often programmed to chase these shoppers and send them pop-ups with discount codes. This works best at specific retail sites, like Gap, Nike, etc.

#2: Create an account at the retailer, put an item in your cart, but don't check out. Instead, log out. Within 24 hours, you will very likely receive a special offer. This is because the website will register your trip as an "abandoned cart," and will try to chase you down to close the deal.

#3: Track prices. This works especially well for higher-end items, such as furniture or appliances. Start your search a few weeks before you are ready to buy. Prices can go up and down based on competing sales, etc. The best sites for this are Capital One and Honey. These browser extensions will alert you to what you can save if you buy the item somewhere besides the manufacturer. Using these is not as lucrative for the cashback feature as Rakuten but you can do both- use these for the comparison shopping and then ultimately link your purchase back to Rakuten to earn those points.

SKIP places like Coupon Cabin and other coupon sites to find discounts. This usually only works for free shipping. There are a lot of bogus codes that will waste your time.

8

FASHION AND BEAUTY

A bargain is not a bargain if it's not what you want.

When shopping retail, you may be tempted to go to the discount stores to get name brands for lower prices. These stores include places like Marshalls, Kohl's, and Nordstrom Rack. Know that all these stores often get the merchandise carried by the large retail chains only if the goods that didn't sell the first time in the non-discount store.

My friends and I went to Loehman's because it was a place to buy designer goods at a large discount. The cheapest place in the store was the Back Room. This was where stuff was heavily discounted. But there was a reason some of this was so cheap. It was the stuff that wouldn't sell. It was the perfectly normal leather skirt that was half off because it was bright purple. I bought some of this stuff because I wouldn't let myself buy things that were too expensive. What happened? I never wore the bright purpler leather skirt.

The worst purchases I have ever made were probably from that store on the sale rack in that back room. I bought a few things there because I could see on the tag that it was $175 marked down from $850 so I thought I was getting such a good deal that I had to buy it. The reality was it wasn't a good deal since I didn't wear them. Now, before I buy something, I think about what else I have that would work with the new purchase and where I would wear this. If I'm struggling for these answers, I don't buy it.

Clothing - Rules to Shop By:

1) If there's something you want and will get value from, then go ahead and pony up. If you really want a pair of tan Uggs, for example, then don't buy knockoffs or the same pair but in ruby red, even if they're cheaper. If you do, chances are that you will still want the tan Uggs and hate the cheapies.

2) Sample Sales: If you are a shopper, you may know that most brands do some sort of sample or liquidation sales. It's almost impossible for them to perfectly plan their inventory. If you are in NYC, Miami or LA, you can find a sample sale every day of the week. Online, there is https://260samplesale.com/. They list in-person sample sales in NY, LA, Chicago, and Miami as well as numerous online sales. If you like a brand, follow them on Instagram and get on their mailing list so you will be invited if they have a sample sale. These sales are great opportunities to get designer goods at a fraction of the price.

I recently got a pair of $300 Cole Haan shoes for $5 at the sale that fit my husband perfectly. The showroom was selling them for so low because they had been worn once for a fashion shoot. Despite the low prices, you still need to check yourself and make sure whatever you are buying is something you need. Even $5 leather shoes are not worth it if they sit in a closet. Most stores take Apple Pay but having cash may give you better negotiating power so it's worth bringing some.

3) Retail sales: Most sales follow cyclical timing. With Black Friday starting now in early October, the whole season is usually a combination of sales through post-holiday sales in January. The best time for summer sales is usually pre-Memorial Day and pre-Labor Day. The point is, that there are always sales. Most of the time a little patience will translate

to big savings. Stores like Tiffany's, Louis Vuitton, and Hermes almost never have sales, but I recommend buying those types of brands used anyway because they hold value very well and are good to wear and resell.

4) Consignment, Used: It is generally smart to buy consignment or gently loved designer clothing/shoes/bags. If it is an item you will be using, buying pre-worn takes away some of the stress of owning such expensive items. Also, these items tend to drop in value immediately going from new to used but the value doesn't drop again after more use if the item is kept in good condition.

Poshmark and The Real Real are top sites for finding great deals on used luxury goods but there are many others. For men, Grailed is also very popular. It's also smart to sell your items on these sites, as they will give you more generous credit than cash to use towards your purchases. This can be a good way to keep your shopping under check because you are exchanging something in your closet that you don't want for something new(ish) without spending money.

My stylist friend is in favor of buying one new outfit a season and selling an older outfit to try to offset the cost. She says it keeps her wardrobe current and feeling fresh to have a trendy outfit for a few months and then recycles it. If you are doing this, it's smart to buy a name brand for better resale.

Other consignment sources- In many big cities, Goodwill has their Goodwill boutiques where you can find almost all brand name items, many with tags. If you are traveling outside the major US markets, that can be an excellent opportunity to find consignment merchandise for less than in the cities. Search Yelp for secondhand/thrift stores or ask locals the best source for these stores.

Don't forget to look on Nextdoor and Facebook Marketplace for designer goods sold per piece or at local estate sales.

6) Shop the classics: I have Jill Sander tall black boots that I bought 25 years ago that I love. I also have black dresses, sweaters, and pants from

years ago that I still wear regularly. Many other items that I loved for a minute have come and gone. For me, black clothing has endured over the years and through the trends. Find your piece, style, or color that holds your heart, and then feel free to invest in them.

7) Depending on your job, if you have to dress regularly for work events, it may be worth paying for a subscription service like Rent the Runway. They have great deals to join and your accountant may even say you can write it off as a work-related subscription service.

No matter how you shop, remember your outfit is not the most important thing about you. I have a friend whose college freshman daughter worked at a high-end boutique. She had a nice discount and bought so many clothes from the shop that she spent way more than she earned. Suddenly buried in debt, she was asked out by the most popular guy at college and she had nothing to wear. As punishment, her mom refused to buy her anything. Finally, the girl broke down and bought something simple on Amazon. She couldn't afford to get her hair blown out like she usually did. Instead, she wore it up. She went to the dance feeling like Cinderella after midnight. However, everyone told her how great she looked, and her date loved her hair because she looked natural. She even went swimming after the dance because she wasn't worried about ruining her blowout.

My husband's roommate had a tuxedo in his closet for years. Turns out he had gone to a wedding and rented this tux, but overslept and couldn't return it so he just paid for it. I used to work in entertainment publicity and got to go to some black-tie events. Once we were invited to an Oscar party, so he borrowed the roommate's tux. The Oscar party was attended by Brad Pitt, George Clooney, and Billy Bob Thorton, among others. My husband was approached by several people who commented on how great his tux looked. It was an After Six rental from Arnold, Maryland that had probably been worn at proms for decades.

The point is that money is not the only ingredient to looking good.

Rely on your taste and style to pull off your look. There are many ways to look your best without spending a lot of cash.

Makeup and Skincare- In terms of makeup and skincare, the major drugstore brands have giant research and development departments and have products on par with the luxury beauty/cosmetics brands. Look at brands like ELF and The Ordinary for simple and inexpensive basics. The Ordinary offers products that are simply one ingredient like Hyaluronic Acid, period. The packaging is plain and they do no marketing so they charge lower prices. Don't get lured in by holiday makeup sets unless splurging on a holiday makeup set makes you so happy and gives you new things to try.

Nails- Short, clean manicures are cheap and last well. It takes about 15 minutes to do yourself weekly and will save you hundreds of dollars a year. Do your friends want to get manicures/pedicures? Have them over and do each other. It is hard to paint your dominant hand. If you do like going to the spa to get a pedicure, shop around before you pick a place. Some salons offer lower prices M-Th when they aren't as busy.

Jewelry- I recommend you only spend a minimal amount for lower-quality trendy pieces. It's a lot less to worry about and you really cannot tell the difference. Pay for real metal for the parts that touch your body — think chains, earrings, and rings. Jewelry is incredibly expensive to insure so it is usually not worth it. Since that is the case, only buy jewelry that you can afford to lose.

Hair- If you are doing single process color, you can do that at home. Not only do you save money, but you also save time at the salon. There are subscription services like Madison Reed and ESalon that offer subscription services for a hefty discount. The other good thing about these subscriptions is that you are not spending money on transportation to get to the store or salon and you are removing temptation from buying other items while in a store. If you are a blowout addict, remember the cost of these services can add up. Best to save these treatments for special occasions. It is also worth investing in a good hair dryer and some straightening products to recreate this look at home. Again, it works very well to blow out hair with a friend because it's almost impossible to get the back and back underside of your hair perfectly yourself.

Men tend to get their hair cut more frequently so your best bet is to look for a chain like Hairzoo, Supercuts, or Fantastic Sams where you can get a punch card after so many visits and maybe a free cut on your birthday. I know they don't sound cool but you can usually look at yelp reviews and find a good stylist there.

ONLINE SHOPPING SCAMS

After saving and spending so carefully, the last thing you want is to be scammed. If you are buying from Facebook Marketplace, Craigslist, or any other group, there are many ways you can protect yourself from a couple of the most common scams.

The shipper bait and switch:

A few years ago, I found a patio table at a price that was too good to be true. The ad claimed that it would be shipped from China, so that was a red flag. I ordered it anyway and got a shipping confirmation. This allayed my fears and I waited patiently for the table. It never came. Weeks later, I messaged the company with no response. I called the credit card that I paid with, and they reimbursed me for the charge. Another week passed and I got a tracking alert that the package was arriving. I ran out to the truck and they handed me a tiny envelope with a mask in it. By sending the shipping confirmation, they were able to buy themselves time. Yes, I did get my money back but if I had paid with a debit card, Venmo, or Zelle, I would have been out of luck.

Be extra careful using Venmo and Zelle. I've often found tickets online to a concert or game at a price that's too good to be true. I hope that the deal is real, however, it rarely is. The scam they play is to insist you pay via Venmo. Unlike credit cards or PayPal, Venmo doesn't offer any protections. Once you've paid, scammers can disappear with your money. This is a different story if you meet up in person and have the item in hand. However, the Venmo-me-upfront scam is almost always bad news.

9

WEDDINGS

You may be at or approaching that age where it seems like everyone you have ever met is getting married. My general advice is to always go to a wedding that you're invited to if your schedule and finances allow it. My husband and I are still friends with many people who we saw get married, and it's important to us and to them that we were there. You also usually will have a great experience at a wedding — the location, the party, new people to meet. Not to mention a nice dinner and an open bar. Even destination weddings might not end up being that expensive. It will be a net loss for you financially, but I argue that the overall benefits are worth the cost. As you can imagine, I have suggestions for how to maximize your experience and keep your expenses as low as possible.

Wedding gifts

You don't have to impress someone by spending a lot on their wedding gift. If you can find a personalized gift that's reasonably priced, then go for it. If you're buying something off their registry, then always try to buy as early as you can. If you do, you can find something at a moderate price that will mean a lot to the couple. I have a fish serving plate that my college friend bought us that was probably only $40, but every time

I use it I think of her. If you wait until the last minute, you'll get stuck buying something stupid or expensive or worse, something stupid and expensive. Get in early and buy something sensible that the couple will actually use.

Guest Attire and Travel

When you are planning to attend a wedding, be sure to consider attire for the wedding and any related events in your estimate of what it will cost you. If you're most comfortable in a suit, buy a nice suit that you can wear to multiple weddings (change it up with different color shirts and accessories) and if you prefer dresses, it's best to get a simple neutral-colored dress you will be able to wear again. If you love the idea of something more festive/colorful/unique, this could be a great time to try out one of the clothing rental services from Chapter 8.

If you are asked to be part of the wedding party, you'll likely be on the hook for a tuxedo rental or dress purchase, engagement party gifts, bachelor/bachelorette trips, and bridal shower gifts. Make sure you're aware of those costs before accepting the honor. If you have to buy a dress, it's worth the time to check Poshmark. Since people don't usually re-wear dresses after being in the wedding party, many end up there for sale.

Also, if you do decide to attend a destination wedding, be sure to pay attention to room block deadlines. Better yet, book as soon as the information is released to be sure you get a spot at your preferred hotel. Weddings often get discounted room blocks so the wedding rate should be the best. That said, don't forget to double-check the hotel website and another search site (Google or Booking.com) to ensure you can't beat the wedding rate. If you're going to a wedding alone, it's great to get a friend to split a room with you since a room with two doubles is usually the same price as a room with a king.

Maybe you are getting married yourself. Weddings are magical special days — and a huge scam. A florist might charge you $500 for 25 table arrangements, but a *wedding* florist will charge $1000. A photographer might charge you $1000 for a 2-hour photo shoot, but a *wedding* photographer will charge you $5000. If the perfect wedding has always been your dream, then get ready for a pricey day. However, if you have a limited budget or prefer to keep your costs down, there are opportunities to cut some corners. Here are some of the significant wedding expenses:

Venue: The cost of the venue can be one of the most substantial expenses. This includes the rental fee for the ceremony and reception spaces. This is also probably one of the most important pieces of the wedding. Can you do the ceremony and the reception in the same spot? If you can, generally that will save you money over having two different venues- one for each. Start from the most important one and then go from there.

Catering: This includes the cost per plate, bar services, and any additional catering fees. Caterers usually charge per person and a seated meal will generally cost you more than a buffet. Also, all those pretty passed appetizers on a tray are expensive, too, so you may want to limit those if you are serving a full meal. Also, daytime catering will usually be less expensive. Lunch items tend to be lower priced, and people are likely to drink less alcohol.

Speaking of alcohol, making a signature drink is one way to save a significant amount of money. Often these drinks can be made in batches so they are easier to serve which takes pressure off the bar so you can have less bar staff. Also, they use less alcohol which means you will be paying less, and most importantly, you don't want your guests to be trashed if you aren't offering transportation.

Photography and Videography: Capturing your special moments is important, and professional photographers and videographers can charge a significant fee for their services. Look for someone earlier in their career who is looking to get recommendations and material for their portfolio.

Attire: This includes the wedding dress, accessories, and attire for the groom, bridesmaids, groomsmen, and sometimes even parents. Most bridesmaids and groomsmen will pay for their own dresses/rentals, but just because you're passing off that expense doesn't mean you shouldn't be budget-conscious. There are plenty of ways to save money for your guests who will certainly be thankful.

Wedding dresses: I bought a brand-new dress I thought I would pass on to my kids. I saved it for years and I eventually donated it. There are sites like Borrowing Magnolia where you can rent a wedding dress for significant savings. Try sample sales or wholesale shops for great deals, as well. Another good option is to buy a simple (inexpensive) dress and splurge on custom alterations to fit your personality. If you want to buy new, shop in the winter or summer when designers release their new lines, so stores discount the older lines to make room.

Entertainment: Hiring a band, DJ, or other forms of entertainment can be a very high cost. For our wedding, we hired a DJ for the reception but a friend volunteered to play piano at the reception which was perfect and beautiful. Do you think music is the most important? If it is your priority, you may want to hire a top band and cut back on the food or the flowers.

Flowers and Decorations: Floral arrangements, centerpieces, and other decorations can add up quickly. Consider going to the flower mart if you have one in your city. Also, think of re-purposing the flowers for the ceremony and reception. The bridesmaid bouquets can be unwrapped and popped into vases for the reception.

Invitations and Stationery: When I got married I hired a calligrapher to address envelopes and had invites embossed. You can save a good deal by designing and printing your wedding invitations, save-the-dates, and other stationery items through a digital printing site.

Wedding Planner/Coordinator: Many couples assume that they have to hire professionals to help plan and coordinate their wedding. These services can be incredibly expensive. If you don't want to take on this responsibility yourself, you might have a family member or friend who would be happy to step in. I went to a wedding recently where the father of the bride planned everything. If you don't have a "Dadzilla" (as this planner dubbed himself), think about giving each member of your wedding party individual responsibilities. If one of your ushers works as a bartender, ask him to be in charge of planning your beverage services and to come up with your signature drink. Your bridesmaid who graduated from film school would probably love editing your wedding video for you. You can tell them that their helping out can be in lieu of a wedding present, so now you're all saving money!

Transportation: Renting transportation for the bridal party is expensive but this is one area where you can find ways to save. You probably already know that it's smart to pre-book an Uber Black to drop you off and pick you up later instead of paying for a limo service for many hours where the car will be sitting. Maybe your uncle is a car guy – ask him to rent a cool car to drive you to and from the ceremony.

Wedding Cake: If you have a friend who is an expert baker, you might want to ask them to make you a cake. This is also one time never to use the word wedding when you are shopping for a cake because it jacks the price up immediately. YouTube has hundreds of videos of people turning cheap grocery store sheet cakes into beautiful wedding cakes.

Favors and Gifts: Providing gifts for guests and bridal party members is often an overlooked additional expense. I think guest gifts are unnecessary unless you have a special idea that is thematic or meaningful. Consider giving your wedding party personalized cards instead of kitschy keepsakes. I once received a silver container as a gift, but inside was a note from the bride telling me how much she admired me. The note means the world to me, and I have no idea what I did with the silver container. If you do go the wedding gift route, Etsy has plenty of great ideas. I personally love monogrammed silk pillowcases as a bridal party gift.

Accommodations: If guests will be coming in from out of town, you'll need to block hotel rooms. Don't just pick one hotel. Some people want a nice place to stay, while others won't want to spend too much. Give your guests two or three hotel options. Hotels will generally offer a cheaper rate since you're bringing them so much business. Also look around for AirBnB's in the area where groups of friends might want to stay. Party houses are great locations for people to gather before and after your ceremony - much better than the expensive bar in the hotel lobby.

Hair and Makeup: Hiring professionals for hair and makeup services for the bride and bridal party can be a major expense. However, this is not a category to skimp. Having professional hair and make-up will take away pre-wedding stress. They are also critical to how your pictures will turn out, and the pictures are the main things that last from the wedding.

The engagement ring: People have different feelings about diamonds. If your bride has always wanted a diamond ring, by all means, go for the bling. Definitely ignore the old mantra that a ring should cost three months of your salary. That was made up by the diamond industry a million years ago. Like all of the categories, you need to prioritize what is important to you and spend on that.

Consider having a ring made instead of buying it retail. Especially if you live close to a big city, there is likely a jewelry district where jewelers sell to the public for close to wholesale prices. A friend of mine lost an earring that her husband had bought for $8,000 for the pair. I suggested we go downtown and ask the jewelry district jeweler to replicate the remaining earrings. She thought they would charge her $3-4,000, but was thrilled when they only charged her $600. She immediately introduced her husband to the jeweler in the jewelry district and asked him to only shop from there if he was purchasing jewelry. Every time she goes back to this new jewelry dealer in the district, her prices have only decreased because of her loyalty and past spending. All this to say, if you have a photo or can do a drawing of a ring that you might like, it is easy enough for a jeweler to make it for you. If you think someone is going to be buying a ring and proposing to you or if you are shopping to propose to someone, maybe enlist a friend for help buying a ring. I had such a friend who knew my taste so well and I'm grateful that she approached my husband and offered to help him buy me a ring if he was going to propose. He took her up on the offer and I still love my ring.

10

EXERCISE

If I were limited to one sentence in this chapter, it would be to encourage you to walk and/or run as much as you can for your health, happiness, and wallet. I could also put this advice in the transportation section because not only do you save on transportation, you get your exercise at the same time.

Walking is also a great way to spend time with friends that doesn't involve going out and spending money. Research shows that men in particular are more likely to open up emotionally in side-by-side conversations rather than in a face-to-face conversation. There is something about being side-by-side where you aren't staring into someone's face so people tend to share more comfortably when walking together. I have had some of my best conversations with family and friends while on walks.

You are also much more likely to meet people walking in the park than if you are driving, taking public transportation, or even biking. Walking with a dog ups that exponentially. If that appeals to you but you don't have a pet, consider volunteering on NextDoor or putting an ad on Rover to combine your exercise and as a way to make some extra money.

Walking is great for overall fitness and can be done almost anywhere.

You get to know a place walking and will discover so much more than you would notice from a vehicle.

Since walking briskly covers your cardio, the other part of fitness you would need to make a complete regimen would be strength training. Fortunately, there are many great free workout videos on YouTube where you can get a full range of exercises for the purchase of a few weights.

If you have trouble motivating and doing an at-home workout, consider signing up for ClassPass. I recommend Class Pass over a traditional gym membership because even though it is a recurring charge, there is no initial down payment and it gives you more flexibility to put it on hold if you travel, get sick, etc. The classes are usually heavily discounted from what they charge and you can often invite friends to join you for free. If they sign up, you get points and money added to your account.

If you like yoga, many yoga studios do special community classes for free or low cost. Search online and sign up for their mailing list. Hotels also offer free classes through their websites and sites like Eventbrite as a way to get people into the hotel and to try to get them to go to the restaurant.

Think of other free outdoor activities like beach volleyball or tennis. Equipment can be expensive, but it's pretty easy to find things like used rackets on Facebook Marketplace. Most cities have tennis courts at the public schools or public parks which are available for free or low cost. It's a fun way to get together with friends or a date for a low investment. The same is true for golf. Although golf has a reputation as a very expensive sport with memberships at the fanciest private clubs costing upwards of $100K, there are also public courses in most cities and these courses often have specials on certain days for low-priced community golf. My kids used to play a local public 9-hole course for $1 on Tuesdays in the summers.

There are many things I dislike about gym memberships. First of all, they can be incredibly expensive. They usually come with long contracts. Often, too, people tend to allow these recurring fees to continue, even if they aren't regularly going. This expense tends to be emotional (guilt) rather than fiscally responsible.

Maybe you're a gym rat who goes to the gym 5 times a week. I'm all for that! I have a friend who spends 3-4 hours per day at his gym, both working out and socializing. He's getting more than his money's worth. Whatever your goals, try to be as realistic as possible when you consider a gym membership.

Most big cities have YMCAs, which are typically the best deals. They offer full weight training, gyms, swimming pools, fitness classes, etc. They aren't swanky, but they are a great bargain and offer nearly the same services as any top gym. As an example, the YMCA in downtown Chicago is about 1 mile from the trendy Equinox. The Y charges $31 per month for young people, and Equinox is $405 per month for their top level membership.

Peleton, Tonal, Bowflex or any of the home gym companies tend to operate on the same model as gyms. They demand a big fee up front, then try to milk you for as much monthly fees as possible. I have a lot of friends who are devotees of Peleton and get amazing motivation from their instructors. They're paying through the nose for it, but they have great abs. Like gym rats, I'm on board if you're getting your money's worth. However, it's the people who spend $2,000 on a spinning bike and $200/month for the monthly subscription, then use the thing as a place to hang their clothes that drive me crazy.

If you need motivation, don't use a long-term gym contract to spur you along. Find a work-out buddy who's at the same fitness level as you and who has similar goals. People are naturally competitive. If your workout buddy loses 3 pounds, you're going to try to lose 4 pounds the next week. FitBuddies, Workout Buddies and MeetUp are just a few of the websites out there that can match you with someone who can push you to reach your goals. This is great way to network, too.

Personal trainers are way too expensive for my taste. However, they can be a lot more effective than going to the gym and doing exercises incorrectly. If you don't have much physical fitness experience, a personal trainer can give you some good fundamentals that will be extremely valuable both at the time and in the future. Most trainers have peak hours and then have no clients during the middle of the day. If you can manage it, try to negotiate with a trainer to train during their downtime at a lower rate. Or consider an on-line trainer. This will give you the motivation and instruction, and is typically much cheaper than in-person. Of course you'll need your own equipment and location, but can be very effective.

11

ENTERTAINMENT

Movies- always take advantage of the promos at your local theater chain. For example, AMCs nationwide have $7 (at the time of publication) movies on Tuesdays. If you go to the movies every week, they also have a group called A-List where you can see up to 3 movies/per week for roughly the price of two movies. This has a 3-month minimum so sign up when you are most likely to use it. If you like blockbusters, summer is probably your season. If you prefer more artsy fare, more likely that winter will be your season because that's when studios put out their awards hopefuls.

Streaming/music subscription services- I prefer to churn these services, dropping one for a while and picking up another. You miss out on new release TV shows, but it's easy to catch up. There's certainly no reason to carry Netflix, Hulu, AppleTV, and Prime at the same time, unless you watch a lot of TV. I'll admit that I've had my kids ask me if we have ESPN+, and I've said no, only to find out that we were paying for it for months. Make sure you know what you're paying for. Sign up for something like Rocket Money which will help find all your subscriptions and help you manage them. Make a deal with yourself that you only ever have a certain number of subscriptions and you can watch everything on that or those services and then move on to the next one. When you do it in a rotation, you will save money and services rarely pull their content off the service.

Live theater- Most theaters have student and community discounts. Look at their education or outreach pages. Tickets are usually discounted for weeknights or matinees. If that timing is an option for you, this is often a good choice.

Museums- Most cities host a day of the year when all museums are free. Most museums will also host free or discounted evenings, primarily to attract a younger audience. Go to the websites of your favorite museums and sign up for their emails so you get notified when they have specials. You often have to reserve in advance.

Sports- If you love one team, you will get the best deal usually if you buy season tickets because exchange fees are generally waived. If you are buying single tickets, depending on the profile of the game, tickets can go for more or less on the resale marketplace. It's helpful to look for sellers who are selling directly. They save on fees and often just want to get rid of tickets more than make a profit. Always try to negotiate a lower price unless they are priced low already. Be polite about it and you don't need to give a reason.

Libraries - Don't buy books when you can check them out from your local library. Libraries also offer all kinds of things, such as museum passes, classes, board games, access to genealogy websites, musical instruments, etc. Get a library account and look into what your local library has to offer. The Libby app and other library apps connect your Kindle or iPad to your local library and e-deliver your books.

Comedy Shows- I'm a fan of comedy shows. I love the raw energy and unpredictability. You can pay big bucks for touring comedians. But the best bang for your buck is weekly or monthly shows of local comedians. These feature up-and-comers but also attract big-name people who want to try out their new material. My husband and I have been going to a local Monday night show and we get to see 7-8 comedians per night, most of whom are very funny. I signed up for a website months back and regularly get emails offering discounted $5 tickets.

12

PETS

Pets are wonderful. They bring so much joy to your life. I could gush about my dog all day long. But this is a book about saving money, and unfortunately, pets can be very expensive.

The first rule for saving money on pets is to adopt instead of buying a pet from a breeder. Don't be influenced by some pets you see on social media. There are so many adorable pets who need homes. You will be spending so much on a pet that there is no reason to spend on a breed. If you do have your heart set on a particular breed, look for rescues for that particular breed. It may take more time but you can usually find almost any breed for free or low-cost adoption. They may not be a baby but that's OK because the bigger medical costs usually come at the beginning or end of life so if you are tight on funds, consider adopting an adult.

If you really cannot afford a pet, borrow one. Offer to pet sit or dog walk or volunteer at a local shelter. Fostering is a great test run so you can understand firsthand how much time and money a pet needs. I have a friend who "shares" his neighbor's dog. He takes their dog on long walks and has the dog over for long periods. She basically gets a free pet whenever she wants. For the owner, this is a great way to give the dog more activity. If you have a friend or neighbor with a dog, offer to take the pup for a walk.

If you are going to get a pet, know that cats are generally less expensive than dogs. They eat less, usually need fewer toys and treats, and it costs considerably less for any care they might need. For our cat, we usually leave him at home while we travel. We hire a local teen to come by once a day to check on him, pet him, feed him, and clean the litter box. This can be had for as low as $10/day. Dog care will usually cost $100/day, whether your board or have someone petsit.

There are a few ways to save on pet costs. Check if your employer has any pet discounts. Many companies offer discount pet insurance as well as memberships to boarding/daycare facilities as part of their benefits. Even if pet insurance ends up being pricier than you'd like, it does protect you from being in the horrible position of having to decide to pay thousands of dollars or not get treatment for your pet.

There are also newer pet membership programs and, if you get in on the ground level in your city, the introductory rates are often quite enticing. I was an early adopter of Modern Animal and got my first year for $50 instead of $150. Even paying full price, I have found it saves money since I can go to the vet as many times as needed. I especially recommend this if you have a puppy or are a first-time pet parent. When I got my first dog, I worried about everything and I brought her in a total of eight times that first year. The app gives you access to a vet on call. This was invaluable for calming me down after my dog got scared and jumped away from a large dog and then started limping the next day (turned out to be a pulled muscle) or when she ate a power bar out of a backpack.

If you work out of the house for full days and need a dog walker or if you travel, there are ways to save on dog care. Consider trading services with a friend, especially if their dog and yours get along well. I connected with a friend a few years ago and our dogs are very good pals. We trade every time one of us travels. Last year her dog stayed with us a total of

66 nights and our dog stayed with them about the same. That would have been at least $3000 each of us would have spent on boarding fees.

The same could be done for walks. It's easy enough to walk two dogs so if you have a neighbor, perhaps you can take turns for dog play dates or walks.

If you need to hire a professional to care for your pet, look at Trusted Housesitter. This app lets you choose from a group of members who are happy to stay at your house for free in exchange for taking care of your pet. There is an annual membership fee but if you aren't renting or trading your home when you are gone, this gives you the next best value out of your home. If you want your pet to go elsewhere while you are out of town, I recommend looking on the open marketplace at Nextdoor.com or Rover instead of your local pet hotel. It's going to be less expensive and usually more individualized care. In short, it is generally a better experience for your pet.

13

TRANSPORTATION

Saving money on transportation feels good to me because I consider it one of the more boring categories, almost as dull as a utility. Still, it is a necessary part of getting around and doing the things you want to do.

Cars

Most cities are dominated by cars. To decide if you need a car, factor in the costs of buying a car, gas, maintenance, insurance, and parking. Once you get a monthly total, it is worth looking at whether it is worthwhile to have a car at all or if you would prefer to spend that same amount on public transportation, walking, biking and/or rideshare/taxis. If you are working from home and mainly going out at night, you may find that you are Uber-ing a lot anyway, especially if you might be drinking.

Lots of people have long commutes and need a car, but there are still plenty of ways to minimize the cost of your ride.

There's a general saying: buy items that appreciate and rent/lease items that depreciate. Cars depreciate - there's an adage that a brand-new car loses thousands of dollars just by driving it off the lot. Leasing, however, isn't always the best route.

The most savvy financial move for car ownership is usually to buy a used car, take care of it, and keep it for a long time. For this, it's best to get a car still under warranty. Even just buying a dealership demo car with low mileage will save you a good chunk of cash but offer that new car smell and protection in case you buy a lemon.

There are exceptions to the always-buying rule. If you have a business and can designate your car as an expense to your business, that is a good time to consider leasing. Also, if you really love cars and it is important to you to drive a nice ride, leasing allows you to switch out your car for a new one every few years.

Electric/Hybrid Cars

Electric cars are more expensive, right? Not so fast....

Electric cars have better resale value, cheaper operating costs, and are less likely to get stolen. They don't have catalytic converters to be stolen and they don't need oil changes.

A great advantage to buying electric is incentives and tax write-offs. Every state is different, and the rules constantly change, but the latest is a $7500 federal rebate on many electric cars.

And the environment.

No brainer.

I'm a big fan of walking as exercise because it can double as your way of getting around. It's not going to be a surprise that I'm also a fan of biking. Biking is one of the most efficient modes of transport, especially if you are traveling less than five miles. You can get a bike on Facebook Marketplace for less than $100 and save on gas, parking, etc. If you are traveling or only need a bike once in a while be sure to check your credit card as a few of them offer free Citi bikes.

When you are ready to trade in one car for another, it's smart to get an offer from the dealer and one from CarMax, but both will almost for sure give you an offer well under the car's value. Instead, consider selling it yourself. I sold my mother's Subaru for $2000 less than she paid for it new, even though it was 5 years old. If she had sold it to CarMax, she would have netted $5,000 less. You may be tempted to sell your car to a place like CarMax because they make it very easy, but it's worth it to try selling it on your own first. Just be sure to follow the local DMV policies about title transfer and if possible go to the bank WITH the buyer to do the deal in cash or with a bank check to make sure you aren't getting a bad check.

Rental Cars

If you do need a rental car, make sure you are looking through your airline and/or credit card company because it is usually a category where you are likely to get bonus miles for booking. Be aware of the benefits of your credit card - my credit card automatically insures all of my rental cars, eliminating the expensive insurance they try to sell you at the counter. Rental agents always push hard to up-sell you insurance and other upgrades. Understanding what you need and don't need will minimize extra expenses.

Also, be sure to check Expedia or Priceline first. Identify the best deal on those sites and then go directly to the car rental site and check their prices. For example, if Budget is the least on Priceline, go to Budget and look at their promotions and price out the car directly with them. You can often get a better deal by booking directly. Also, the cancellation policy is often more flexible.

While considering the big car rental companies, it is also worth it to look at Turo for peer-to-peer car lending. It's usually less expensive, albeit for a slightly older car. Another nice thing about Turo is that these cars all have reviews which is more than you are ever going to get in terms of knowing the specific car you will be driving.

Always make the smart choice about rental cars. Especially if you are staying in a city, be sure that you need one, as parking is often very expensive at city hotels. Factor that cost in when figuring out how much you will be spending. I always call my hotel ahead of time and ask what they charge for parking; I also ask if they have self-parking that is cheap or even free. Even if they say no, do your research. I've parked on nearby streets while staying at a hotel many times. A three-block walk versus a $68 nightly valet fee? No contest. Just be sure to read all the parking rules! You know how I feel about parking tickets.

Parking

No surprise again, but I hate paying for valet parking. The fee and the tip are just too much. I almost always skip valet. Sometimes places are geographically arranged so that there is no other option. It's down a mile-long drive, it's a wedding, etc.

Always look for alternative options. If you plan, you can almost always find alternatives. I've used apps like Park Hero and Parking Buddy and paid 10% of what friends paid for similar spots. For example, parking spots for the Taylor Swift concert were selling for $100, and those lots were all jammed. My friends and I parked three blocks further away on the street for free.

For a football game once, I drove my husband and son to the game dropped them off, and then picked them up. We saved what would have been $100 on parking or Uber as well as avoiding the hassle of waiting hours for an Uber after the game.

Public Transportation

Public transportation is always going to be the cheapest option. Mass transit, however, is not always the fastest or most convenient. These days "last mile" options — scooters and rideshare bikes — are everywhere, so this has helped bridge that gap. Check your credit card as some have partnerships and give you free last-mile transport as part of your benefits. If you can get by with just public transportation and no car, you'll free yourself of a significant expense and responsibility.

Carpooling

Cars are not meant to be used for one person. Share rides with friends, family, or colleagues. Carpooling can help split fuel costs and reduce wear and tear on your vehicle. And, it's more fun to sit in traffic with someone else. My kids have made some of their best friends carpooling. It's a good bonding time and a good way to warm up into an experience and then time to rehash, debrief, etc. Next time your friend says she is going out of town, ask if she wants a ride to the airport. Then, hopefully, she will offer you a ride the next time you go to the airport.

Biking

Bicycling is sort of the perfect hybrid between driving and walking. It adds variety if you are tired of walking and gives you a different view and it's significantly faster than walking. E-bikes are a fantastic option for commuting because a lot of people typically avoid bikes because they don't want to get sweaty on the way to work. E-bikes eliminate that concern.

Car Care

If money is tight it is easy to put off that oil change for a few more months or skip the tire rotation or car wash. However, doing these maintenance chores can improve fuel efficiency and prevent costly repairs. Cars are expensive and a well-maintained car can be significantly more valuable when it comes time to sell it or return it on a lease.

Driving Efficiency

Adopt fuel-efficient driving habits, such as avoiding rapid acceleration and braking, maintaining a steady speed, and keeping your vehicle well-tuned. These practices can improve gas mileage. Choose a less busy time to drive when possible. Time spent idling in traffic still uses gas but doesn't get you anywhere.

Gas Prices

Gas prices can vary by location and station. Even gas stations close to each other can have drastically different prices. Use apps like GasBuddy to compare gas prices in your area and choose the most cost-effective option. Also, take advantage of discounts on gas offered through most grocery rewards programs.

Remote Work

If your job allows, inquire about the possibility of working from home part-time. This isn't for everyone and certainly not every job. However, even working from home once a week can reduce your commuting costs and time. There are also lots of fully remote jobs available these days. Hone your search to remote only and see what you can find.

Ride-Share

If you frequently use ride-sharing services like Uber or Lyft, compare prices, and consider using shared rides or pooling options to split costs. This may be a time to consider a credit card with ride-sharing benefits. For example, Amex includes $15 monthly credits for Uber (ride or Eats), as well as a special $35 credit in December.

Insurance

Review your auto insurance policy regularly to ensure you get the best rates. Consider raising your deductible or bundling insurance policies for potential discounts. If you are going to be traveling, know the rules. Some insurance companies don't need people named on the insurance policy unless they "turn the key" a certain amount of times per month. Be sure to check alumni associations or places like AAA and Costco which may have better rates.

Avoid Unnecessary Trips

Plan your errands to minimize the number of trips you need to make. Combining multiple tasks into one outing can save both time and money.

Discount Programs

Check if your employer, local government, or community organizations offer transportation discounts, such as subsidized public transit passes or bike-sharing programs.

Employee Perks

Some employers offer transportation benefits, such as subsidized public transit passes, parking discounts, or commuter assistance programs. Some companies will not only pay for your monthly mass transit, but also pay your for not parking in their lot. Take advantage of these offerings if available.

Refinancing/Downsizing

If you have an auto loan, explore options for refinancing to lower your monthly payments. RateGenius and Autopay are two good sites to see if you can get a better rate. Additionally, downsizing to a more fuel-efficient vehicle can reduce overall transportation costs. If you are in a lease and are close to the end, you can usually approach the car company a few months earlier. You are likely to get a retention offer on a new lease or purchase at this time because they want to keep you as a customer.

14

HOUSING

In most big American cities, rent will run you 25-35% of your salary, which is a ton of money for something that gives you no equity or tax breaks. You get those things when you buy a home, but owning a home is some straight-up adulting. To buy, you'll be expected to pay 20% upfront to avoid private mortgage insurance. Then there are the closing costs which can run from 2% up to 6% of the loan. You need money, you need long plans to stay in one place, you need the commitment to pay a mortgage for 30 years.

Rent or Own?

The decision on whether you should rent or buy depends on various factors. Usually, renting makes sense when you are unsure if you will stay in an area for longer than a couple of years. Reciprocally, it makes sense to buy if you plan on sticking around and have the coin.

To buy a house, you need to have a significant upfront cost for the down payment, closing costs, and ongoing mortgage payments. When my father bought his first house, his boss at the time told him, "Now I can take you seriously." What he meant was that he now considered my father an adult, a long-term employee. Taking this leap into full-fledged adulthood is a big one that should not be done lightly.

Renting is easier. If your toilet stops working, you call the owner or management company, and they have to deal with it. If you get a job in a different city, you break your lease and off you go. Before we got married, my husband used to say he was a renter, because he never wanted the commitment or responsibility. After owning our house for 20 years, he thinks renting is a waste of money and has gotten slightly okay at home repairs, including fixing toilets.

Advantages to home ownership

When you rent, you're not making any investment. When you own, you build equity over time. Equity is the amount that you own, or what you would get after paying off your mortgage after selling. Building equity allows you to see more of a return on your investment when it's time to sell your house.

Another important consideration is the tax benefit of owning a home. On your income taxes, you can choose to take the standard deduction which is currently $13,850 for single filers and those married filing separately, $27,700 for those married filing jointly, and $20,800 for heads of household in 2023.

Itemized deductions, subject to certain dollar limitations, include amounts you pay for mortgage interest on loans up to $750,000 (or more if you bought the home a while ago). If you are a high-earner, writing off this mortgage interest can have worthwhile savings and add a compelling reason in the buy column.

Renting has lower upfront costs, but your rent payments will likely increase over time which can eat away at your disposable income.

Market Conditions

Buying: In a stable or rising real estate market, buying can be a good investment. In a declining market, it might be hard to sell. Interest rates play a big part in the decision to buy a home. At the time of publication, rates are hovering about 7 percent which is historically problematic for home purchases. If the market declines after you buy, you can find yourself "upside down" or owing more than your house is worth. You also might have trouble selling your house, then you're stuck with mortgage payments on a house you don't want and that's not earning you any money.

Renting: Offers flexibility, especially in a volatile market. You can easily relocate without the hassle of selling a property.

Long-Term Plans

Buying: If you plan to stay in an area for an extended period, buying provides stability and potential long-term financial benefits.

Renting: If you're unsure about your long-term plans or need flexibility due to work or personal reasons, renting might be a better fit.

Maintenance and Repairs

Buying: You're responsible for maintenance and repairs, which can be costly. However, you have control over your property.

Renting: The landlord typically handles maintenance and repairs, relieving you of some responsibilities.

Market Rent vs. Mortgage Costs

Buying: Your mortgage payment may be comparable to or lower than local rental prices, making buying more attractive.

Renting: In some areas, renting might be more cost-effective than buying, especially when factoring in maintenance costs.

Credit and Qualifications

Buying: Requires a good credit score and financial stability to qualify for a mortgage.

Renting: Generally requires a slightly lower credit score and may be more accessible for those with limited financial resources.

Equity Building

Buying: Builds equity over time, which can be a valuable asset for future financial endeavors.

Renting: Does not build equity, but it provides flexibility and freedom from the responsibilities of homeownership.

Personal Preferences

Buying: Gives you the freedom to personalize and modify your home as you see fit.

Renting: Offers the ability to easily change living arrangements.Ul timately, the decision depends on your personal and financial goals, current circumstances, and the local real estate market. It's essential to carefully evaluate your options, considering both short-term and long-term implications. Consulting with a financial advisor or real estate professional can provide valuable insights based on your specific situation.

Buying a Condo vs. A Single Family Residence

If you do decide it is the right time to buy a home, one of the first decisions will be whether you will buy a single-family residence or a condominium. Some of the pros and cons of selecting a condo are below.

Pros:

More affordable

Enhanced Security

Condo owners don't need to worry about outside maintenance, such as landscaping, snow plowing, or other repairs because the homeowners' association (HOA) typically takes care of it.

Cons:

Privacy: Condo owners share walls and common spaces with other residents, which can lead to a lack of privacy

HOA fees: Condo owners must pay recurring HOA fees that cover maintenance, amenities, and other costs

Rules: Condo owners must follow rules that govern the entire building, which can limit personal freedom and affect things like pet ownership and renovations

Slower appreciation: Condos tend to appreciate more slowly than single-family homes

Housesitting

This is great way to save money on rent (and earn some cash) if you want to stay somewhere and take care of pets. TrustedHousesitters and Rover both have resources to match you with homeowners. For a fee, you could essentially stay for free all over the world.

There's a lot of talk recently about passive income (basically earning money without really working for it), and one of the best ways to do this is by using your home. If you already have a home or apartment, there are multiple ways to monetize it.

Home Exchange

This platform allows you to share your home with other members without dealing with taxes, restrictions, etc. This platform can be joined for a modest fee currently set at $150, but available for less during promotions. Other homeowners stay in your home for points or a reciprocal exchange. All members are verified and members review each other so the site offers another level of trust. Also, you are often staying in each other's home so people tend to be very respectful. It creates a community and a better feeling than a VRBO/Air BnB.

VRBO/Airbnb

These can be options for you to take advantage of and earn money from your home when you are not there. You only need to be aware of local restrictions and the fact that you will need to pay taxes. You will also need to manage the transactions and check in/outs and clean yourself or through an agent.

ADU

An ADU (additional dwelling unit) can mean anything from renting a room out in your house to building a free-standing rental on your property. Before going down this road, you need to check the local codes and laws (not just for building, but for renting). This can become a job because now you're in charge of fixing things and maintaining a nice rental. However, having a renter is an excellent way to cover your housing expenses and hopefully earn you something on top of that.

15

TRAVEL

I considered writing an entire book about saving on travel but decided to include this shortened version in this book. I have a long history of travel and this is my favorite chapter. I love planning trips, even if for someone else. And I love finding great travel deals. Tourism is a business that fluctuates with whims and seasons, so there's always great opportunities to find incredible deals.

Travel has always meant a lot to me. I was bit by the travel bug early. My first trip abroad was a family trip to Portugal when 9 years old. It was the first time I stayed in a hotel with an in-room safe and I thought it was the fanciest thing I had ever seen. I had my first lobster bisque and chocolate souffle. I carefully selected a small wooden boat as my souvenir from a picturesque fishing village and cherished it for years.

I had the good fortune in my early 20s to work for a company where we got 40% off airfare. We used to take weekend trips to Europe to go to nightclubs and walk around the city all night. I've been to Australia, Japan, Africa, Tahiti and to Hawaii and Europe many times. I've been lucky enough to travel in first class for work and I have also done basic Eurail passes and slept in bug-ridden hostels.

My advice is to travel as much as your schedule and budget allow. My husband taught me a saying- "You always remember your travels - even bad trips. But you never remember why you didn't go on a trip."

I have been able to find great deals on travel for as long as I remember. It's not uncommon for me to check into a hotel and the clerk to ask if I'm a travel agent because the rate they see for my room is so low. It happened on my honeymoon in Bora Bora. The hotel couldn't believe the rate. He said, "This is less than my employee rate. I have no idea how you got this."

When planning a trip, I always ask friends for advice. People love sharing their travel memories, and it's always best to have someone you trust tell you what museums or restaurants are worth the visit. .When it comes to accommodations, I always look for "cheap and cheerful." I often pick the least expensive option that will make me happy. That way, if I'm torn between two choices, if they really are equal, I choose the less expensive option but if I know I will be happier at the more expensive option, I do that.

For example in Spain, it was just my two kids and me so the priority was safety as a single mother traveling alone in a country where I didn't speak the language. I picked based on location, knowing we would be taking public transportation and would want to be close to the city centers. Though it wasn't expensive, I loved our hotel in Barcelona. It was old and charming and very clean and the staff went out of their way to make us feel welcome. That hotel had more character than a typical big-brand hotel, even a luxury chain. Plus, for a trip like this one, the hotel isn't that important because I plan to be out exploring the city and only at the hotel to sleep. When I'm going to a resort where I will be spending the bulk of my time on property, I prefer five-star service and facilities and don't care so much about unique charm.

I see some people take their whole families on luxury vacations. I don't think young people should travel in first class. Just like working as a waitress teaches you how to treat wait staff, I believe traveling in coach grounds you and allows you to appreciate it later. My point is that you should embrace cheap travel – think of it as not only saving you money but also giving you opportunities for adventure and character-building.

Learning how to travel richly will save you tons of money throughout your life and enrich your life in many ways. You may hear the term Travel Hacking. This is a term for learning to travel extremely cheaply. It is often focused on getting first-class travel for free/cheap using points but can cover all sorts of travel savings. I've tried tons of travel hacks, and here are some of my favorites:

1. Be an opportunistic traveler. Map out places you want to go. Build out your travel goals and set your financial limitations. Understanding what your habits are and what you hope to do are the keys to success in this game. Subscribe to newsletters so when one of your places comes on sale, you're ready to pounce. Start with **Thrifty Traveler, JGOOT,** and **The Points Guy**.
2. Start looking as soon as a trip is on your radar. The earlier you start looking and the more time you spend looking, the more likely you are to find a good deal.
3. Look regularly. Deals change, so you need to keep looking even after you've booked a trip. If airlines lower their prices, you can get a refund for the difference.
4. Be flexible if you can with airports and dates. Use Google Flights, Kayak or Hopper to do searches, leaving dates or destinations flexible in order to find bargain options. The last time my daughter came home from NY on the Sunday after Thanksgiving she couldn't be flexible with dates because she had class Monday morning. However, she was flexible in airports. She ended up flying out of Ontario, which was only 20 minutes farther than LAX for $320

cheaper.

5. Take advantage of free stopovers to combine places and see more at the same time. Places in between continents often have free stopovers like Iceland, Ireland, and Hawaii, and national airlines tend to offer them as a special promotion to visit that country.
6. Try to piggyback work trips so that you can combine. If work is sending you to Atlanta for a meeting, ask them to fly you to Miami on the way back instead of home. Now you get a trip to Miami and you only have to pay for your one-way flight back. Doing a three-leg trip will often save you quite a bit of money.
7. Many credit cards include travel insurance, which is a great benefit and cost savings. Check to see if your card does. If not, and you plan on traveling a lot, it might be worth considering getting a card that does.
8. Learn how to calculate point redemptions so you know when you should pay cash for travel and when you should use your stash of credit card points (See Chapter 4). I have included a point calculator which you can use to figure out when to spend and when to save your point. Try to resist using them when it doesn't shake out. .
9. For hotels, it pays to be loyal. I love charming boutique hotels but when I do stay at chain hotels, I'm loyal to Hyatt. I think they have the best hotels and the best loyalty program. Hyatt, Marriott, and Hilton all have strong programs where every dollar spent is converted to points you can redeem for free rooms and other perks. If you can link their partner airline, you often get bonus credit or higher status (i.e. American and Hyatt accounts can be linked, as can Marriott and Uber and Lyft and Hilton) Also, look out for partner bonus offers with airlines and credit cards at hotels.
10. As mentioned, a great way to avoid paying for hotels at all is HomeExchange. For an annual fee, this website allows you to earn points by hosting guests in your house and can spend those

points staying in other members' homes. We have had great success sharing our home and staying in members' homes all over the world. We have met nice people and saved a ton of money. We recently stayed in a condo in Breckenridge over the New Year's holiday week and the family that owned the condo stayed in our house while we were gone. We even left each other our cars at the airports so when they landed at LAX and we landed in DEN we each had a car to drive for a week for free. The home and car would have been about $8K if we had to pay for it. Since it was free, it took the sting out of paying for lift tickets, rentals, and pricey meals on the mountain.

11. Consider companion passes. These let you bring along a companion for free once you're qualified, usually by earning enough credit card or frequent flyer points. Hawaiian, Delta, American Airlines, and British Airways all have different versions of these deals. Southwest also has a really good deal. You need to earn 135,000 points to get the pass so the best way to do this is if you get a new Southwest card you get the sign-up bonus and maybe get a business card as well.

16

BILLS, INSURANCE, UTILITIES, TAXES

No way around it — paying bills is boring. I included a chapter on it because it's an important (if boring) aspect of your finances. The more organized and smart you are with things like bills, taxes and insurance, the more money you'll save yourself and the better you'll feel. When I first started living on my own, I used to wake up in the middle of the night worried I forgot to pay the power bill. Some simple skills will help overcome that anxiety.

Student Loans

Over 13% of the population has outstanding student loans, and the debt totals an average of $37K for Federal loans and $55K for Student Loans. If you are one of these people, this can cripple your monthly budget. If so, be sure you look into loan repayment plans and loan forgiveness plans. There is currently a federal SAVE (Saving on a Valuable Education) plan that is the newest income-driven repayment (IDR) plan.

https://studentaid.gov/announcements-events/save-plan

Like other IDR plans, the SAVE Plan calculates your monthly payment amount based on your income and family size. In addition, the SAVE Plan has unique benefits that will lower payments for many borrowers. If you have an exceptionally low interest rate, you may not want to change anything but it is worth considering.

Beyond SAVE, there is also a newly approved loan forgiveness plan that will completely forgive up to 20K in loan debt for qualified students. You also may qualify for loan forgiveness if you work for a non-profit or in a public service role.

If you have been through these steps and have gotten your loan down as much as possible, your monthly loan payment will simply need to be a fixed cost that you allocate right away every month.

Health Insurance

As of 2024, health insurance is mandatory in 5 states. It is not a federal law. However, even if not mandatory in your state, it is crucial to cover medical expenses. If you don't get health insurance through work or school, know that the Affordable Care Act (Obamacare) has made it considerably more affordable to have insurance.

You may be able to stay on your parent's plan until you turn 26, or you can explore individual health insurance plans. If you are not yet earning a high salary, it is likely you will qualify for government subsidies. These are often generous credits that offset your cost. **Check Healthcare.gov for rates and qualifying details.**

Healthcare expenses, especially in a serious situation, can quickly add up and be catastrophic financially. It is not worth the risk to be uninsured, or for that matter, under insured. Healthcare.gov has a questionnaire to help you figure out which plan is best for you.

Most companies large and small offer some form of health insurance for their employees. Learn as much as you can about what your company offers and take as much advantage as you can.

The first decision you will probably have to make when choosing insurance is if you want to sign up for an HMO or a PPO.

The key thing to note is that HMOs work very well within their network of doctors. However, if you need to go to any doctors out of network, you will not have any coverage at all. HMOs get a bad reputation because many doctors do not accept them but if you have a good network of doctors who do accept yours, it is a very cost-efficient plan.

If you get a PPO, you will likely have a large deductible before your insurance starts paying for a lot of services but with good or even decent insurance, "in-network" preventative care is usually free to you. Take advantage of this by finding doctors you like in your medical plan's network and getting medical check-ups, dental cleanings, flu shots, etc. A lot of people in their 20s don't bother to get check-ups, but catching something early can not only be best for you health-wise but also save you a lot of money.

With a PPO, you have the option to go to any doctor who is out of your network and they will cover some portion but it is much less.

The most common insurance money mistake is going to an out-of-network doctor without realizing it. Some offices are better than others in telling you that they are out of network but it is always your responsibility to make sure you are going to an in-network provider because then they have a contracted rate and it limits your liability. If you go to an out-of-network provider, at best the insurance company will cover a portion of the visit. At worst they won't cover it at all. It's not enough to say, "Do you accept my insurance?" This is like asking if they accept money. You need to ask, "Are you in-network with my insurance?"

There are plans that offer you an opportunity to have a Health Savings Account (HSA) along with your health plan. These are awesome because HSA is funded with tax-deductible dollars and the money grows tax-free and is not taxed when you withdraw it as long as it is used for health care expenses.

Take advantage of employee incentive programs with your insurance or otherwise. There are often cash bonuses for completing online health training, logging your exercise, or other programs.

Dental and Vision Insurance

These types of insurance cover expenses related to dental and vision care, which are usually not covered by health insurance. It is usually worth it to have some sort of low-cost dental insurance or a Dental Savings plan that gives you discounted prices on dental services with participating dentists in the network. Always max out the number of cleanings you can do each year. This helps dental hygiene of course, but it also trouble shoots problems before they become big and costly. Many vision plans will pay for screen glasses, which are great to have considering how much time we spend in front of our computers every day.

Renters Insurance

If you are renting a home or apartment, renter's insurance can protect your personal belongings in the event of theft, fire, or other covered perils. It also provides liability coverage. If everything you have is inexpensive and you don't have an unusual risk of theft, you can probably skip this expense. However, if you have expensive personal belongings, paying a few hundred dollars per year to protect thousands of dollars of goods can be the prudent choice. In this case, it's helpful to do the cost/benefit analysis.

Homeowner's Insurance

If you own your home and have a mortgage, it is mandatory to have homeowner's insurance. Get at least three quotes to make sure you get the best deal. Once you select a provider, look closely at the declaration page. The deductible is the place you will save the most money. It is worth it to have a high deductible because you likely won't report a loss on your homeowner's insurance unless it is really expensive.

Case in point: I have a friend who just got robbed. Her deductible was $5000. They took about $6000 worth of jewelry and purses. She could have reported it but then they would have raised her prices by $500 a year. In two years she would have been out more money than if she had not reported it, so she didn't report.

Another friend had a beautiful lakeside summer rental house. She had a bad experience where she was sued for an accident that took place on her property. Her homeowner's insurance saved her from financial ruin.

Home/Rental Repairs

One great thing about renting is that repairs are generally the responsibility of the landlord. If you own and need a repair or service done at your home (think lawn, plumber, etc), always get multiple quotes. The simpler it is the more I like to negotiate or shop around. For something like a gardener, look for the cheapest.

Universal Life Insurance

I found it really strange when I started researching finance books that there are a number of books completely focused on universal life Insurance.

Universal life insurance is a flexible permanent life insurance policy that allows policyholders to adjust premium payments and death benefits while accumulating cash value based on market interest rates. Recently it has gotten a lot of press as a way to save for college. Here are some arguments for and against using universal life insurance for college savings:

Arguments for universal life insurance:

- Tax Advantages: One of the primary arguments in favor of universal life insurance is the tax advantages it offers. The cash value of the policy grows tax-deferred, and withdrawals can be made tax-free up to the amount paid in premiums.

- Flexibility: Universal life insurance policies often offer flexibility in terms of premium payments and death benefits. This flexibility can be appealing for individuals with variable incomes or changing financial situations.
- Creditor Protection: In some cases, the cash value of a life insurance policy may be protected from creditors. This can be advantageous for individuals who are concerned about potential financial liabilities.
- Death Benefit: If the policyholder passes away, the death benefit can provide financial support for the beneficiaries, including funds for education expenses.
- Lifetime Coverage: Unlike term life insurance, which covers a specific term, universal life insurance provides coverage for the policyholder's entire life, as long as premiums are paid. This can be beneficial for long-term financial planning.

Arguments Against Universal Life Insurance:

- Cost: Universal life insurance policies can be more expensive than other forms of life insurance, such as term life insurance. The premiums for these policies often include not only the cost of insurance but also fees and expenses.
- Complexity: Universal life insurance policies can be complex and difficult to understand. The combination of insurance and investment components may make it challenging for individuals to make informed decisions about their policies.
- Investment Risk: The cash value of universal life insurance policies is often invested in sub-accounts that are subject to market fluctuations. If the market performs poorly, the cash value may not grow as expected, impacting the policy's performance.
- Opportunity Cost: Critics argue that the returns on investment

within a universal life insurance policy may be lower compared to alternative investment options, such as 529 college savings plans or other tax-advantaged accounts.

- Fees and Charges: Universal life insurance policies may come with various fees and charges, including mortality and expense charges, administrative fees, and surrender charges. These fees can erode the cash value and reduce the overall return on investment.

After doing extensive research, I think there are some benefits to the product but, because of the high fees, it really only works best as a college savings strategy if you start pretty much as soon as you have a baby. If you haven't done it then, you may as well skip it. We did not use this strategy for our kids and don't regret it.

When considering universal life insurance as a tool for college savings, it's essential to carefully evaluate your financial goals, risk tolerance, and the specific features of the insurance policy. Consulting with a financial advisor can help you make a more informed decision based on your specific circumstances. **The people who sell this life insurance are usually 100% on commission so they are quite aggressive. It is smart to speak to another impartial source before making a decision.**

Auto Insurance

If you own a car, auto insurance is legally required in most states. It typically includes liability coverage, which pays for damage you cause to others, as well as coverage for damage to your own vehicle. To save on auto insurance, make sure you are getting all the discounts. There are lots of options to find deals: your college, AAA, your job, etc.

1. Compare rates:Get at least three quotes. Make sure you are comparing the same levels of coverage. You should have high enough coverage limits to protect you. I recommend at least 100/300

or 250/500. These numbers refer to the liability coverage limits provided by an insurance policy, where "100" represents $100,000 for bodily injury liability coverage per person, and "300" represents $300,000 for bodily injury liability coverage per accident.To keep your rates low, increase your deductible from $500 to $1000 across the policy.

2. Don't pay for rental car coverage. If something happens to a rental, you'll figure it out. This is an excessive expense in my opinion.

Life Insurance

While life insurance might not be a top priority for someone in their 20s or 30s, it's worth considering, especially if you have a family. Life insurance can provide financial protection for your loved ones in the event of your death. If your employer has coverage, that is usually sufficient. The other consideration is an annuity. People have written books and books on this. Some people think life insurance is a total scam. Others think it's a smart tax dodge. Like anything, there is no right answer.

Disability Insurance

Disability insurance provides income protection if you become unable to work due to a disability. This type of insurance can be essential to cover living expenses if you're unable to earn an income. Many companies offer this as a benefit. Generally, I wouldn't tell someone to buy this type of insurance unless they were in some sort of higher risk profession.

Insurance is always customized, so it's important to assess your specific needs and circumstances when deciding which insurance coverage you want. Additionally, insurance needs change over time, so it's always good to review your coverage periodically. Consult with insurance professionals or financial advisors to get personalized advice based on your situation.

Utilities

If you are renting you may be limited in terms of decisions you can make about utilities. However, if you own, you can make efforts to reduce consumption and increase efficiency. Here are several tips to help you save:

Energy-Efficient Appliances: If you are selecting new appliances, actually look at the energy ratings. If you already have appliances, you still may want to consider replacing older appliances with newer, energy-efficient models. Energy Star-rated appliances can significantly reduce energy consumption.

- LED Lighting: Switch to energy-efficient LED light bulbs. They use less energy and last longer than traditional incandescent bulbs. This sounds small but they last for years.
- Unplug Devices: Even when not in use, electronic devices and chargers can still draw power. Unplug devices or use smart power strips to cut off power to multiple devices at once.
- Programmable Thermostat: this will regulate your home's temperature. Set it to lower or raise the temperature when you're away or sleeping to save on heating and cooling costs. The Nest is a great example.
- Seal Leaks: Even if you are renting you are most likely paying for your own A/C and heat so make sure that you inspect your home for air leaks around windows and doors. Ask your landlord to seal any gaps or cracks with weatherstripping or caulk to prevent drafts.
- Proper Insulation: Adequate insulation in walls, ceilings, and floors helps maintain a consistent temperature, reducing the need for heating and cooling.
- Regular HVAC Maintenance: I recommend annual cleaning/maintenance of your heating, ventilation, and air conditioning (HVAC) system. Replace air filters and clean vents, and make sure your

system is running efficiently.

- Water Conservation: Install low-flow faucets and shower heads to reduce water consumption. Fix any leaks, and consider using a water heater timer to heat water only when needed. Tank-less water heaters are the most efficient, so consider going that route if you can, but older electrical systems won't support them.
- Energy-Efficient Windows: Double-pane or triple-pane windows can help improve insulation and reduce heating and cooling costs.
- Adjust Water Heater Temperature: Lower your water heater's temperature to around 120°F (49°C) to save on energy costs. This is typically sufficient for most household needs.
- Energy Audit: Consider conducting a home energy audit to identify areas where energy efficiency can be improved. Some utility companies offer free or discounted energy audits.
- Time-of-Use Plans: Check with your utility company about time-of-use plans. These plans often offer lower rates during off-peak hours, encouraging you to use appliances when demand is lower.
- Monitor Usage: Keep track of your utility usage. Many utility companies provide online tools or apps that allow you to monitor your energy and water consumption.

By implementing these strategies, you can make your home more energy-efficient and reduce your overall utility costs. It's often the combination of small changes that can have a significant impact on your monthly bills.

Taxes

Taxes are a considerable expense and most people would agree there is nothing fun about spending on taxes.

The top tips to save on taxes:

1. Retirement savings: Max out your retirement plan options. I know it doesn't feel fun to save for retirement when that seems like such a distant consideration. However, knowing that you're saving money for the future instead of just giving it away to the government makes it a little more fun. If you haven't already maxed out an employee contribution at work, make sure you make the largest contribution allowed under the law. This IRA limit goes up a little bit every year but for 2024 it is $7K. If you don't have a retirement plan through work, you still want to make annual contributions. Charles Schwab or Fidelity can help you set up the best plan and make sure you're hitting your max.
2. Filing: If you have one W-2 or are making less than $75,000/year, do your taxes with Turbo Tax or one of the free/low-cost online tax companies. If you earned more than 100K or if you are self-employed, you probably need to hire an accountant. Interview a few before you hire one. Ask their policy for questions during the year. Some charge an hourly fee and some don't charge for questions. This can make a big difference. Expect to pay anywhere from $200-$1000. This amount is deductible on your taxes. Just because the accountant is a professional, it behooves you to completely understand your taxes. First of all, you must sign your returns, attesting that you are legally responsible. Second, accountants are busy and many just respond to what the clients ask/need. Don't be afraid to check in with them and ask questions like "Are there any other deductions I might qualify for?" or "Should I do anything differently to set myself up for a better tax outcome next year?"
3. Stocks: Stocks are a great way to invest , but do come with risks and tax liabilities. If you are making money off your investments, you will want to make sure you are tax-loss harvesting in December every year. Tax-loss harvesting a strategy where every year you re-balance your investments in a way that serves your investment

strategy but also minimizes your tax burden. When you sell losing assets of a dollar value and then sell assets that have a profit of the same amount, you can use whatever monetary loss to cancel out any gains of the same amount, eliminating any tax liability. As an example, say you want to sell your Apple Stock and you bought it for 10K and now it is 30K. That would be a 20K gain. If you don't sell anything else, you would have to pay tax on that 20k at the rate of your ordinary income if it is a Short Term Capital Gain (meaning you held it for less than one year). If you held it for more than a year, you would have to pay tax on a more favorable Long Term Capital Gains tax rate which can be between 0-20% but falls at 15% for most filers. Let's say you held it for more than a year. You would owe 3K on your 20K. Now, let's say you also bought some other stocks along the way and they were losers. If you bought Zoom at the height of the pandemic and you paid 25K, it could well be now down to 5K. That is a 20K loss. You could sell it the same year as your apple and that 20K loss balances out your 20K gain and now you don't owe any tax.

4. Charitable donations: If you will be itemizing your deductions you want to make sure to include these. Remember to donate any unwanted items to an organization like Goodwill or Salvation Army. They'll provide you a receipt with a Tax ID on it. Make sure you keep an itemized list of exactly what you donate as well as an estimated value of the items. When you file your taxes, you will deduct charitable contributions on your Schedule A. Because the donations only make a difference if you itemize deductions rather than taking the standard deduction, it may make sense to lump donations in one year if that will push you over the limit to itemize because to itemize you need to have at least $14,600 to deduct to make it worth itemizing. Save your receipts!
5. Business losses: If you had a great year in earnings, that means

you're going to get hit harder than you ever have on your taxes. But there are ways to mitigate the pain. This could be the year to start your side hustle if it's something you have always wanted to do but it is unlikely to be lucrative right away. You can write off the business loss to offset regular income. For example, if you start a website, you'll need to buy the domain name, build the site, pay for hosting, etc. These costs will hit you long before you make any money, but they can all be counted as business losses that will offset taxes that you owe on money that you did earn. If you do have a business, it's also worth exploring whether you work as an LLC or corp or a different entity if you are making more than about $60,000 a year on your freelance/consulting activities.

6. Write-offs: If you work and are paid as a full-time, permanent employee, at the end of the year you will be provided a W-2 form. Working as an employee, your deductions are a little more straightforward, as you won't have as many business expenses that you can deduct. If you are a consultant or an independent contractor, you will be provided with a 1099 form for your taxes. In this case, there are more options for tax saving strategies so it becomes more important to work with an accountant who works on a lot of the same type of clients. Back when I was an assistant in the movie business I had an accountant who mostly worked with actors. He used to have us write off everything. Makeup, hair, nails, fitness – it was all related to our jobs. I wouldn't recommend this these days as tax laws have changed. Plus, this accountant is now in jail.

17

GET THE MOST OUT OF YOUR JOB

Jobs can give you a lot more than just a salary. Many companies offer things like pet insurance, bagel Wednesdays, and unlimited vacation. It's on you to know what they offer and take full advantage. It's generally understood that benefits (401k, health coverage, etc.) for a full-time employee are worth between 18-22% of your annual income. Therefore you should take as much advantage of your company's benefits as you can. It is amazing how many people pay no attention to their company's benefits. It's a good idea to sit down with your HR person during open enrollment and ask them what benefits you're missing out on. Most HR people want you to use up all the benefits you can, so they will likely be very helpful.

401K- If you work for a company that offers a 401K as part of their benefits, that is the first thing you should prioritize over all other savings. First of all, the way it's automatically deducted, you probably won't even notice that it's being taken out. Second, if they have a company match then it's free money. This is a common benefit where the company matches whatever you contribute up to a certain amount. This is usually set at 10% or 15% or your salary so definitely hit that maximum amount.

Insurance- Generally, employer-sponsored health insurance is some of the best insurance out there. A large portion of the monthly premium payments are usually subsidized by your employer leaving you with a much lower responsibility. Make sure you're getting your yearly check-ups (general, vision, derm) while you have good coverage

ESPP- Employee Stock Purchase Programs. Generally, some people will say not to invest in your own corporate stock. They say you are already working with the company so your fortunes are already intermingled with the company so it's not a diversified bet to also buy company stock. I would say it depends. If you're at a successful national company and you get a discount, then you should probably max out this benefit. Stocks rise and fall, so your company stock might not seem like a winner right away, but over time it will probably be worth it." If it's a risky investment, skip it and spend your investing dollars elsewhere.

Other benefits-Make sure you are taking advantage of all of the benefits working for a company provides. This often comes in the form of discounts at things like health clubs, dry cleaning, doggie daycare, and mental health. Again, be sure to ask if you're missing out on something because companies add benefits all the time. Plus, these benefits are often explained to you on your first day, when you're dealing with a lot. So it's always a good idea to circle back and make sure you're taking full advantage of what's offered to you.

Free coffee, bagel day, etc.- Don't scoff at the chance to get your fill of kombucha, bagels, sandwiches, or whatever on the company dime. That said, companies also will load up on snacks like M&Ms, granola bars, and soda in the break room. ut Remember that healthy food is always best for your body, and you will pay in other ways if you are constantly indulging in starches or sugars.

Expense accounts- I know a lot of people dream of having an expense account. There are plenty of stories of people living lavishly on the company dime. In reality, however, it's usually a lot more boring. Most companies will only pay for cheap airfare, cheap lodging, and low-dollar meals, and then you have to keep tabs on it all and submit the receipts like you're a tax accountant. Whatever you are offered, take full advantage. Just remember, this is your career, so don't push the limits. If you are lucky enough to have an expense account, ask if you can put all of the charges on your card and be reimbursed that way. In that case, you accumulate the miles for all of your corporate spending which can be considerable. Be the one to volunteer to put everything on your card.

Vacation- Know what your company vacation benefits are. If you have unlimited vacation which is now the trend, take it because they won't pay you out when you leave so you may as well take as much vacation as you can.If you are allotted a fixed number of vacation days, make sure you educate yourself about how much rolls over, so that you are getting the benefit of all of the time you deserve. If you can only roll over 2 or four weeks, make sure you're using the rest. If you know you are quitting soon, hold on to your vacation days because the company will pay you out for those unused days.

Pay Increases- This is an important part of corporate work life that can add significant money over time. Deciding when to ask for a raise involves careful consideration of various factors. Here are some situations when it might be time to consider asking for a raise.

- Significant Performance Achievements
- Positive Performance Reviews:
- Increased Responsibilities
- Industry Standard or Market Changes

- Employment Anniversaries:
- Cost of Living Increases:
- Company's Financial Performance:
- Positive Relationship with Your Supervisor
- Personal Financial Needs

Before you ask for a raise, be sure to research industry salary standards, gather evidence of your contributions, and practice articulating your case. Choose an appropriate time for the conversation, such as during a performance review, and be ready to discuss how your increased compensation aligns with your performance and the value you bring to the organization.

Getting a raise- Before you get used to the new amount, instead of spending the increase, invest it. If you were getting by just fine before, you don't need the additional money. It is a great time to Pay Yourself First and put that money towards investments or a long-term goal. Splurge on something to celebrate, then start banking more money for your future.

Getting raises and growing in your career is an important part of reaching your financial goals. If your current company doesn't value your contribution, another way to spur them to give you a raise is to get a competing offer. I worked for the same company for the first ten years of my career. Every time I would ask my boss for a raise, she would say, "I would love to give you a raise, but I'm only authorized to give you 5%. If you want more than that, go get an offer." I would go get an offer from an outside company and magically my company would counteroffer and usually match the competing offer to get me to stay.

Knowing When It's Time to Move On

If you are unhappy in your current role and it's about more than the money, start to look for a new role right away. Gone are the days of even staying in a role for a certain amount of time. I have consulted in recruiting for Apple and other tech companies and we didn't look down at people who left quickly.

The general rule still holds that you should switch jobs every 3 years. This is a good length of time at an employer to show that you have demonstrated longevity, but it's also a good time to go after a title increase and a bump in your salary.

You may have heard that it's easier to get a job when you have a job. Well, it seems to be true. There is something about hiring someone with a job that companies seem to prefer. If the candidate isn't employed, it makes the company wonder why they aren't employed, if their skills are up to date, etc.

Applying for a New Job- When interviewing for a new role, there are a few musts. First and foremost, never go negative in an interview. No one wants a bad apple, so always spin even the worst situation into something positive that you learned from. Also, avoid disclosing your current salary. Early in the interview process, you will be asked what you are making or what you are looking for. Try to side-step this question, and instead ask what the budgeted range is. If you tell a company that you're looking for $80-100k, they will offer you $80k. Many states now require companies to disclose their ranges up front, and this knowledge is extremely helpful. Finally, when negotiating for a new job, focus on your base salary. Don't ask for a higher bonus, because those are discriminatory and taxed at a higher rate. Especially, don't focus on chasing a higher title. Being a Sr. Associate instead of just an Associate might sound better, but it won't add anything to your bottom line. It's better to save room for title increases when you're on the job, as this helps when asking for raises. If the company is doing 3% increases, you need a strong justification for asking for more. The title increase is exactly what HR wants to approve a big yearly increase.

Unemployment- I wish there wasn't such a stigma about unemployment. It is money you have put into the system, and there is no reason you shouldn't take that money back out when you need it. If you are unemployed through no fault of your own, you are eligible for unemployment; this benefit ranges from $40-$450/week depending upon what you were earning before you were terminated. The total amount of benefits you can receive in a period without filing for extended benefits is around $11,000. If you do get laid off and need to file for unemployment, do so right away. There is a one-week unpaid waiting period you must serve before you are eligible to get benefits. Hopefully, you will be get a new job before long so you may as well get as many weeks of benefits as you can before you are working again. Pro Tip: always take the maximum benefit you qualify for and do not have the EDD take taxes out. Hopefully, you will be employed again soon so you may as well get the maximum benefit while you need it. Yes, your benefits will run out more quickly but you will end up with more of a payout if your unemployment ends quickly.

18

WORKING ON YOUR OWN

There are multiple ways to earn money. Salaried (also called full-time or permanent) employment is the most common. This is usually when you work for a bigger company and get benefits like health insurance and a 401k. But not everyone has a full-time job. The last chapter focused on full-time roles, so let's take a look at other ways to earn a living.

Independent Contractors

You may be working as a contractor because you're a consultant, you have multiple clients, or your employer doesn't have a headcount for a full-time role. Also, if you are transitioning to a new career, just got laid off, or are building a company on your own, you will likely be an independent contractor. This is often referred to as 1099, which is the tax form you file (instead of a W-2 for full-time staff).

As an independent contractor, your client can't tell you when or how to do your work. They are paying you for goods or services, and can't control how you provide those. They also shouldn't give you things like a laptop, unless there's some propriety software or system that the company requires you to use. As a contractor, you submit invoices, and your client will pay you the full amount, so no taxes are taken out. This means you have to be prepared to pay all of your taxes at the end of the year. You also don't get any benefits, so you're responsible for things like health insurance.

There are both good and bad aspects of working this way. Contractors have nice freedoms. Contractors eat what they kill, make their own hours and don't have to go into an office. However, contractors can be eliminated very easily. At the first sign of a downturn, for example, companies usually cut all the contractors first to save money.

Being an Entrepreneur

Starting your own business is a lot more lucrative, if riskier. I used to work with a marketing leader who was very tight with the CEO, so I thought he was in a cushy situation. However, when I talked to him, he treated his job as just okay. When I questioned him about it, he said, "I'll never get rich here." The simple truth of his statement floored me. But, in a way he was right. His very good yearly salary would give him security and savings, but the job lacked the upside that having his own company could provide. Similarly, when I started going to a cosmetic dentist who had just moved to LA from Israel, I asked him about finding a job, and the concept made no sense to him. "You mean people just take jobs to make money for someone else? Why would they do that?" He started his own dental office and is now a massively successful Beverly Hills periodontist.

There are a lot of wonderful things about working on your own and building your own company. If you have an idea for a company and want to start your own business, do it now. Believe me. When you have large expenses and a family or other commitments, it's harder to take time off to start a new venture.

If you are building a business, you are primarily responsible for how much you work as you are the one to get work and accept it. Generally speaking, entrepreneurs tend to work constantly. I've known people who've done things like launch a tech company, start an accountant staffing agency and open a car wash, and they all said that they were amazed by how much work they had to do.

e No matter what route you choose, be sure that you establish short-term and long-term goals to guide your journey. Having goals can help you stay focused, measure progress, and achieve success.To build your business there are a few key pieces:

Define Your Niche

- Identify your strengths and passions and specialize in that niche.
- As appropriate, use social media to network and promote your services. LinkedIn is the primary place to do this. Many promote their businesses on Facebook, Instagram, TikTok, etc. but it very much depends on the business. For example, a cookie design company looks great on TikTok but an accounting firm, not so much.

Create a Detailed Portfolio

- Showcase your best work in a portfolio that highlights your skills and expertise.
- Provide case studies or testimonials from past clients to build credibility with potential clients. It's ideal to get the testimonials as soon as you wrap a job or in the middle of an ongoing relationship so you don't have to go back to old clients when you are no longer top of mind.

Set Realistic Prices

- Research the standard going rates in your industry and set prices that reflect your skills and experience.

Network and Build Relationships

- Attend industry events, join online communities, and connect with other freelancers.

Continuous Learning

- Stay updated on industry trends, tools, and techniques.
- Invest time in learning new skills to stay competitive in the freelancing market.

Maybe you need or want to make more money now. How do you choose what you want to do? The best side hustles can vary depending on your skills, interests, and the amount of time you can commit.

You probably know more about the gig economy than I ever could. I'm not telling you anything new here but just laying out options to get you thinking. Here are some popular and potentially lucrative side hustles you might consider to boost your income:

Freelancing: Offer your freelance skills on platforms like Upwork, Fiverr, or Freelancer. Best for writing, graphic design, programming, and marketing.

Online Tutoring: If you excel in a particular subject, offer your tutoring services through Chegg Tutors, Tutor.com, or on your own through social media.

Content Creation: Start a blog, YouTube channel, or podcast based on your interests. Once you grow your audience, you can monetize these platforms through advertising, sponsorship, or affiliate marketing.

E-commerce: Sell handmade or unique products on platforms like Etsy or start your online store using Shopify or Amazon.

Affiliate Marketing: Promote products or services and earn a commission for each sale made through your unique affiliate link.

Stock Photography: If you're a photographer, sell your photos to stock photo websites such as Shutterstock, Adobe Stock, or iStock.

Consulting: Offer your expertise as a consultant in your field. Great for business consulting, career coaching, or any area where you have valuable insights.

Online Courses: Use your knowledge of a particular subject or skill to sell online courses on Udemy, Teachable, or Skillshare.

Virtual Assistance: Provide administrative support to businesses or entrepreneurs as a virtual assistant.

App Development: Develop and sell mobile apps. You can offer them on app stores or work on custom projects for clients.

Be wary of influencers on Instagram and other platforms promising you that any of the above ideas and others are the road to instant riches. Mega success in any of these, as well as digital marketing, ebook publishing, and other hot side hustles, is very unlikely. You are best to only pursue one of these hustles if you are genuinely interested in the journey.

If you just need to make some extra money now and don't have time to wait for a passion project to hit?

Here are some more instant gratification options-

Concert Tickets- If you know a show is going to be sold out, it can be worth going on early to get premium seats and resell them. This is especially true if you can get access to presale tickets. The caveat is to only buy tickets you wouldn't mind using if you can't sell them or only buy tickets you know people want (i.e. Taylor Swift). I recently had the opportunity to purchase presale tickets to a popular concert. Knowing that it would sell out and likely sell for more than the face value I bought the maximum number of tickets allowed. I used two of the tickets to take my niece to the concert. I sold the other two to my cousin for face value and I sold the last pair on StubHub. From the profit I made on StubHub my niece's and my ticket were essentially free.

Resale- It can be profitable to buy and resell furniture and other home goods. Some people say that in real estate you actually make a profit when you buy, not when you sell. That means, always try to buy at a good price, especially if it is something you are looking to turn around and sell. Another thing you may have heard is that a new car loses a chunk of its value as soon as you drive it off the lot. That is true for most goods. If you are trying to resell, don't buy new and expect to sell for the same once it's been used but if you buy used and sell used, that can usually be profitable because most designer and high-quality goods will be worth almost the same when you sell whether they are one year old or four years old. Case in point, a table from RH that is worth $2000 new. It may be worth $1200 when you buy it two years old. If you sell it again three years later, you probably could still buy it for $1200 so take care of your stuff. I think it works best to buy brand-name goods, not for the luxury factor but because they hold their value better. Same with cars.

Ridesharing or Delivery Driving: Join platforms like Uber, Lyft, or DoorDash to earn money through driving or delivering food.

Fitness Coaching: Become a certified fitness coach and offer personalized workout and nutrition plans online.

Remote Customer Service: Many companies hire remote customer service representatives. Look for opportunities on job boards or company websites.

Childcare, house sitting, dog walking- I'm grouping these together because they are all caring for something or someone. The best places to find these types of gigs:

Rover- for pets

NextDoor- for pets, housesitting, childcare, etc.

Bambino- for childcare

Before starting anything new, consider your skills, the time you can commit, and the potential for growth and income. It's also essential to comply with any legal and tax requirements associated with your chosen side hustle.

19

INVESTING

If you follow some of the ways to save money in the book, what should start happening? Hopefully, instead of just making it paycheck to paycheck, you will start to accumulate extra money. Once you have some savings, you want to put that money to work for you. Leaving your money in a checking or low-interest savings account is fine, but inflation will eat at any interest you earn, and more importantly, you will be missing out on opportunities to grow your wealth.

You might be excited about investing, but you need to make sure that you've first built out emergency savings. I know that is no fun but you do need to save before you can get to the fun part.

Stock market investing could be considered a side hustle if you are going to focus on it as an income stream. If that is the case, however, you need a lot more training and be prepared to invest a lot of time. Income from stock trading is taxed differently and there is a higher level of risk.

You may be lured by investing schemes on social media, but these returns are mostly exaggerated. Passive buy-and-hold investing is the best way to build wealth with minimal risk.

The downside of investing is the possibility of market fluctuations.

The best type of investing is the boring kind – long-game investing. This means sitting on a stock even though it's down, sometimes by a lot, and this is because most of the time it will eventually go back up. Smart investing therefore means that you'll need to tie up some capital. If you ever need to raise cash fast, it's not ideal to do so by selling off stock and that's because you may be selling when the market is down.

These are the two key segments in investing.

Retirement Investing

Hopefully, you're maxing out your 401K. But what if you have 10% of your salary or 20% of your salary that you'd like to invest? What do you do with the money?

The first thing you want to consider is the annual IRA contributions if you haven't already maxed out your retirement contributions at a W-2 job. For any other contributions, you have a choice between putting your money in an IRA or a Roth IRA.

"Traditional" IRA (pre-tax)- This is a great way to squirrel away money since the taxes on that money are deferred. Hopefully, once you retire and need this money, you're in a lower tax bracket so you don't take as big a hit.

"Roth" (post-tax)- You don't get a tax break when you put the money in, but your investments grow tax-free and when you eventually take distributions in retirement, you don't have to pay any tax.

Which should you choose? Most likely you will have both types of accounts and every year you evaluate and choose the best one for that year.

Contribute to a Roth IRA if your income is lower than you expect in retirement and choose the traditional if your income is higher than you expect in retirement.

Non-Retirement Investing

Retirement investing is anything that is NOT in your retirement accounts. There are many types of investments. You need to consider every investment when you are weighing whether or not it is worth your money.

Here are the primary investments that are important to know when you are starting to grow your portfolio:

Index Funds - These are low-cost bundles that mirror one of the stock indexes, like Dow Jones or NASDAQ. I put these first because if you want to make it easy and save on fees, low-cost index funds are your best bet. Over time, they will most likely beat mutual funds because statistics show that over 15 years, only 6% of actively managed mutual funds beat their corresponding market indices.

Equities (Stocks) – This includes Individual Company Stocks traded on the public exchanges. The three you need to know:

DOW- A stock market index of 30 prominent companies listed on stock exchanges in the United States.

S&P 500- 500 of the largest companies listed on stock exchanges in the United States.

NASDAQ- The second largest exchange. It focuses heavily on tech stocks.

Mutual Funds- Actively managed stock funds that come with higher fees and try to beat the index averages but often don't.

Bonds – These instruments have lower expected returns but also lower volatility. These can include individual company bonds, US Government Bonds, Index bond funds, and actively managed bond funds.

Target Date Funds- These are a common fund type you will most likely come across if you invest in a child's 529 or in your retirement fund because they are set up to transition the set of investments from riskier to more conservative as you approach the date when you are expected to need/withdraw your money.

It's best to keep everything with one low-cost brokerage if possible. The big ones are Schwab, Sofi, and J.P. Morgan. Explore their websites and see which interface or tools appeal to you most. If there is a free introductory session with a money manager when you start off with a brokerage, take advantage of that. Also, take a look at all of their free learning on their site. Most brokerages offer regular webinars where they pitch their actively managed portfolios but they can also help with balancing investments.

Here are some benefits of maintaining a consolidated portfolio:

1. It's easiest to keep track of your investments if you have everything all in one place. There are portfolio checkup tools that can tell you if you are properly diversified, but if your investments are all over the place, the tools don't consider those investments so won't be as accurate or valuable.
2. Brokerages have tools and features that are very helpful, but they are best when all or most of your investments are in one place.
3. There are often bonuses, lower fees, and better rates for larger accounts so it makes sense to consolidate your money.

Here are some terms you'll need to know:

Expected Return – how much you expect to earn by holding the investment.

Volatility (Risk) – the variability of the historical actual return of an investment.

For example, if you purchase stock (equity), you might expect a 10% return over the following year, but the return might be as low as losing 25% (the historical worst year loss of the stock market) or positive 25% (the historical best year gain).

If you buy a bond, you could expect to earn a lower return of say 5%

but the risk is much lower. The most you could expect a bond to go down is historically only about $15.

Whatever your investing strategy, try to take advantage of **Dollar Cost Averaging (DCA)**. Using this strategy, you will divide your total investment into multiple recurring orders, rather than trying to time the market with one large buy. If you are in a good flow with your budget and can set up recurring investments, you will naturally do this. The benefit is that you are more likely to buy when the market is at all levels.

The thinking behind **DCA** is also relevant for selling stock/funds, etc. If you can't decide if it's time to sell, sell half. If it goes up you can sell the other half and make a little more. If it goes down, you will be glad you sold the first half.

"Set it and forget it"

You shouldn't touch money that you have earmarked for retirement, so simply set your strategy and then you only need to check it quarterly. This is often enough that you should start to see some progress but not so often that you are spending a lot of time on it.

Ninety percent of your investments should be in some sort of solid, "stable" growth investments. No more than 5% should be allotted for riskier alternative investments if you want. This would be investing in art, crypto, etc.

Real estate investing is another huge segment of the investing market but I'm not going to get into that here. If you are interested in learning more about real estate, I recommend *The Book on Rental Property Investing* by Brandon Turner as a first read.

20

ACTION PLAN

You've made it this far, so that means you are serious about trying to live a richer, fuller life for less. You may be feeling a bit overwhelmed and hopefully, you have lots of ideas and questions. To get started on the road to financial freedom, you need to take action. Here is a fast action list of ten steps you can take to get yourself in better financial shape quickly:

1. Write down your financial motivations and goals.
   A- What is your why?- Why are you doing this?
   B- What is your what- what are you going to continue to spend on?
   C- What is your who cares- what are you going to stop doing to save?

2. Download the Acorns app. Start shaving off those extra cents and invest them.

3. Make your own coffee. I just bought a used Nespresso on Facebook Marketplace for $50. You can get a French press for less. My son likes cold brew so he got a cold brew maker on Amazon for $20. He makes a batch and it stays in the fridge for five days. Whatever it is, pick your

coffee or tea and try that.

4. Open an investing account. Use the free welcome session to set up a balanced portfolio of ETFs or Index funds and set up some recurring investment of ANY amount. Schwab shares start as low as $5 so there is NO excuse not to allot some amount to this. If you have an existing account already but aren't doing much with it, send a message to the brokerage to see if you can get a call with a money manager to best maximize your investments.

5. Find free ways to have fun. Sign up for the mailing lists for local theaters and museums so you will be alerted of free days or other promotions.

6. Wean yourself off delivery apps. Instead, stock your kitchen with staples, try cooking some meals, and walk to pick up your take-out.

7. Find cheap travel. Get a travel rewards credit card if it's the right time for your credit. Sign up for Thrifty Traveler, The Points Guy, Travelzoo, and The Points Guy. If you have any bucket list destinations, set alerts for low airfare.

8. Cut recurring fees. Use RocketMoney to find subscriptions you should end.

9. Plan a free fun day. Invite friends and family to meet at a beach/-park/hike or a free cultural activity.

10. Share this book! Any journey is more fun and likely to be more successful if you have accountability and a partner. For my own personal financial success, I'd prefer if your partner bought a book for themselves.

But my frugality is too strong - lending/borrowing books is smarter.

There may be times along the way when you say, "It's too hard to save money." That's OK. Saving money and spending wisely are lifelong endeavors. Splurging on things you care about will be much sweeter when you aren't doing it all the time, so treat yourself regularly. Celebrate the good moments and go easy on yourself when things are hard.

Don't feel bad about it but know that it was the exception. The great thing about having a plan is that you have something to aim for when you go astray.

After you have completed the fast action 10 steps, you are well on your way to living richer.

Money is not the most important thing in life. However, if you get better at saving and spending, you will have more time and money to focus on the important things- experiencing your favorite things in life with your favorite people. So happy trails on your path. You've got this!

Made in the USA
Monee, IL
04 November 2026

67383135R00069